Remembering a Mentor

I have benefitted from different mentors at different stages of my life. All of them were very affectionate, considerate and enlightened. Of these, two persons who shaped my attitude to the profession in my days as a junior IAS officer in Bihar were Shri Jagdish Chandra Jetli and Shri Samir Kumar Ghosh.

I first met Ghosh saheb when I was Sub Divisional Officer of Bettiah in the old Champaran district in1969. It was my first independent charge and I had a baptism in fire as the whole subdivision was in turmoil within a couple of months of my joining due to an agitation launched by the Socialist Party and the Communist Party of India for distribution of all vacant government land among the landless peasantry. Shri S.K. Ghosh joined as the Tirhut Divisional Commissioner around that time and decided to visit Bettiah to make an on-the spot assessment of the situation, which was then by far the most serious threat to law and order in the state.

My Collector was not quite confident that a 'Madrasi' greenhorn like me would be able to handle the volatile politics of Bihar and might have made his misgivings known to the new Divisional Commissioner. Nevertheless, Ghosh saheb took an instant liking for me at our very first meeting and his encouragement did a great deal to pump up my self-confidence. His unflappable temperament restored a certain chirpiness among all of us in the midst of the prevailing tension. He took us on a week-end picnic to the Saraiyaman lake where we were joined by his family. Indeed it turned out to be a highly informal outing for all of us with the Commissioner acting as head of the family. Looking back, I realize how important this picnic was in restoring camraderie and cool professionalism in dealing with a difficult situation.

My interactions with Shri S.K. Ghosh sharpened my understanding of the socio political environment in which I was to operate as a civil servant in Bihar. Though I did not have the privilege of working under him later in my career, our personal bonds grew stronger with the passage of time, especially as his son Abhik Ghosh became a very close personal friend. The administrative acumen and instant humour of late S. K. Ghosh set him apart as an exceptional civil servant and his affectionate nature and kind heartedness made him a great human being. The opportunity to work under Shri S.K.Ghosh early in my career was a great blessing for me.

K. Roy Paul
Former Secretary, Government of India
& Member UPSC

In Remembrance

Shri SK Ghosh was the Divisional Commissioner of Chhotanagpur over four decades ago when I joined as Deputy Commissioner, Ranchi. I still recall vividly that Shri Ghosh - who treated me like a son - was always warm, accessible, eminently practical and had a great sense of humour. What I learnt from him in the six months that he was my Commissioner stood me in good stead during my remaining years of service.

N. K. Sinha
Former Secretary, Government of India

Fascinating and Endearing

A fascinating account of a bygone era: one that blends nostalgia with anecdotal analysis. It depicts in graphic detail the dilemma of upright civil servants seeking to avert the creeping influence of excessive political interference in discharge of their principal obligation to maintain security and order amid the growing development focus of post-independence India. Bihar was then emerging from a feudal, hierarchical order into a modern society. In many ways the multiple contradictions in the governance rubric is brought out in this eminently readable book.

The book also highlights the systemic erosion of civil service values of political neutrality, impartial decision making and free expression of views with candour and objectivity. These were and must remain the abiding framework of a permanent civil service, its basic raison d'être.

Samir Ghosh demonstrated in ample measure these values in his dealings with superiors, colleagues and indeed all who came in contact with him. He remains an example worth emulating by succeeding generations of civil servants. For someone like me belonging to the Bihar cadre, it evokes memories of times gone by and the quest for excellence which many talented civil servants like Samir Ghosh sought to assert.

The several complimentary references to my late father T. P. Singh makes this book that much more endearing for me.

A valuable account for political and economic historians.

N.K. Singh
Former Secretary to Prime Minister

In memory of Sri Samir Kumar Ghosh

Samir Kumar Ghosh was an earnest devotee of our revered Guruji Sri Sri Paramahansa Yoganandaji. I recall him reciting in his sonorous voice poems from Tagore as his soul offerings to his Guruji on the occasion of Guru Poornima every year.

He served Yogoda Satsanga Educational Institutions for about 20 years in various capacities. We specially remember with gratitude the years he served as the Secretary of Yogoda Satsanga Mahavidyalaya, a role that he executed with the pragmatism honed from his brilliant career in the Indian Administrative Service. His ever-youthful vigour, spirited dedication and the sagacity of his innate quiet nature that was so much a part of his personality, were qualities that impressed and inspired those who worked closely with him.

His dedicated life, lived for one and all, brings to mind the following words of our beloved Gurudeva: "Feeling the sorrows of others and reaching out in order to make them free from further suffering, seeking happiness in the joy of others, constantly trying to remove the wants of increasingly larger numbers of people -- this is being sacredly selfish... He lives to love his brethren, for he knows they are all children of the one God... So when he does anything for himself, he can only do that which is good for all. He who considers himself as one whose body and limbs consist of all humanity and all creatures certainly finds the Universal All-Pervading Spirit as himself."

Swami Smarananda Giri
General Secretary
Yogoda Satsanga Society of India

Those Were the Days, My Friend

Reminiscences of a Civil Servant

Samir Kumar Ghosh

KNOWLEDGE WORLD
KW Publishers Pvt Ltd
New Delhi

ISBN 978-93-86288-24-0

Published in India by Kalpana Shukla

KNOWLEDGE WORLD

KW Publishers Pvt Ltd
4676/21, First Floor, Ansari Road
Daryaganj, New Delhi 110002
Phone: +91 11 23263498/43528107
Marketing: knowledgeworld@kwpub.com
Editorial: jose@kwpub.com
Website: www.kwpub.com

2011 FPBA BEST PUBLISHERS AWARD (ENGLISH)

Printed and bound by Bhavish Graphics.

Contents

- Foreword ix
- Filial Tribute xvii
- Prologue xxvii
- Initiation and Some Foretastes 1
- Independence and Some Early Trends 11
- My First Sub-division: A Package Deal 19
- The Golden Years 31
- The Descent Begins 39
- Scenes from the District: Factions in Action 43
- Kosi Project Department: Some Rare Experiences 51
- The Night Descends 57
- United Front Government: The Ramgarh Affair 63
- Some Experiences of the United Front Government 73

- First President's Rule: A Succession of Governments 79
- From Pillar to Post 87
- The Land Beautiful and Endless Exploitation 97
- Waves Upon Waves and a Happy Ending 105
- In Far Away Tripura: A Fitting Epilogue 119

Foreword

TSR Subramanian*

"The more things change, the more they are the same."
"Gresham's Law – the bad coin forces out the good"

In 1942, Samir Ghosh as a provincial civil service probationer stepped into the office of WG Archer, District Magistrate and Collector of Patna District – and thus begins the story. This is enough to take any civil servant - serving and retired - down memory lane. How many PCS or IAS probationers can forget their very first encounter with the Collector on the day they joined the district for training? The delightfully written memoirs of Samir Ghosh in a sense can be re-lived by thousands of PCS and IAS officers from every corner of India, covering the usual 35 years of public service. The venue, locale, dramatis personae and actual events would vary in detail, but the essential understanding of the job of the civil servant would remain the same as projected by Ghosh. Herein lies the commonality of the experiences of civil servants, the steel frame that has held the country together for over seven decades – a frame that may be somewhat rusty and rickety now, but which still continues to play its indispensable role.

---

* Mr. TSR Subramanian is a former Cabinet Secretary to the Government of India.

Ghosh joined the Bihar provincial civil service in 1942, five years before the country's independence. He took voluntary retirement at the end of 1975, having seen three decades of service in the state in independent India. The Paul Appleby Report on India's Administration was written in 1953, when Ghosh was still a relatively junior officer. Appleby characterized the then Bihar administration as among the best in India; today any insider, or indeed, any dispassionate observer, would probably categorise Bihar as one of the worst administered states in India. Ghosh, as a young officer, was witness to and describes the process of steady decline of governance in Bihar, giving some snapshots of events that have driven it to its present stage of despair. His memoirs give more than a hint – indeed, he paints a sketch about the origins of the fall – without laying the blame on any one individual, by merely describing the depressing scenario as he saw it unfold from different view posts. No doubt, the likes of Lalu Prasad and other Bihar politicians played their destructive role in accelerating the decline and fall of the Bihar administration at a later period – Ghosh was, in fact, in some measure, an eye witness to the politicization of the state apparatus during the three decades that he served the state. Reading between the lines, he has made an excellent diagnosis, without formally naming the disease. He provides an insider's view "of the moves of state level politicians in their quest for power, which soon reached a stage where these desperate men freely staked the interests of the state for their partisan political ends" … "despite all the sacrifices made by our leaders during the struggle for freedom, these clever politicians' basal weaknesses got the better of them as the spell of power and spoils of office took hold". Elsewhere, Madhav

Godbole has written of the intellectual dishonesty displayed by the Indian national leaders in the years immediately preceding our independence – logically leading to the present depraved state of our politics and polity. Ghosh has seen the Bihar version of the same disease and provides an explanation as to what has gone wrong in our management of national affairs.

Early in the memoirs, there is already a reference to Lord Wavell, the then Viceroy of India, visiting Patna. And what does he do? He visits the interior of crowded mandis to get a first-hand picture of the rampant black market in the textile trade and the operations of the district administration in regulating the supply of the rationed commodity. Can one recall a single recent instance of a Chief Minister or Minister or Secretary to government visiting the local bazaar or school or hospital to acquaint himself (or herself) with the quality of the field administration? Apparently Viceroys of yore saw themselves as public servants, in contrast with latter-day politicians who saw themselves as Emperors born to rule. The administration in the field, at the implementation level, is at least as important as that at the level of policy making. Ghosh already refers to 'big importers stashing away cloth consignments from the mills, whole-sellers forging accounts to feed the black market, big thefts in stores, the ubiquitous politicians demanding special favours, in a low key to begin with and getting ever more strident, influential socialites demanding favours beyond the rationed quotas' – the rot, it appears, had already begun.

There is a reference to communal incidents and tensions – all these in the context of events accompanying the freedom struggle.

Which young district officer of that era did not experience them in every state of northern India? However, communal rage had not yet acquired the political colours and dimensions which they did in subsequent decades, where communal issues were used as fodder for vote-bank politics. The clear picture that emerges from the account of those early days implicitly reflects the fairly large degree of amity between the main communities, with the occasional mischief-monger raising his head to vitiate the atmosphere. Since then, communal issues have been promoted to the realm of highly excitable vote-bank politics – so much for the democracy that we have tried to sustain and nourish.

That Ghosh spoke his mind on most occasions, without fear or favour or being too politically correct, is something that clearly emerges from the narrative. The implication also is that most civil servants of the time were able to freely express their views on all official matters, and they were invariably supported by the official hierarchy. What a sea-change between then and now – particularly in the states, where officers are willing to crawl when asked to bend and seniors are ever-willing to sacrifice their junior officers without any hesitation. How many District Magistrates or Secretaries now stand up to protect their subordinates from politically-inspired false allegations and save them from summary transfers. Surely the political class of those days thought twice before removing an officer from his post. How many officers in the entire state of Uttar Pradesh stood up to defend the young sub-divisional magistrate Durga Nagpal against humiliation and injustice heaped on her a couple of years back?

In the same vein, Ghosh speaks with great fondness and admiration about three chief secretaries with whom he had worked – L. P. Singh, Triveni Prasad Singh and P.K.J. Menon. It is remarkable to see the attention given by successive chief secretaries to ensure that district, as well as secretariat level officers, were not trifled with. Contrast this with today. How many deputy collectors and magistrates in the districts would even remember the name of their chief secretary and, even if they did, would be willing to record for posterity the leadership qualities of their superiors. Ghosh, at numerous places in the narrative, speaks of the propensity of politicians to interfere in routine administrative matters to gain political or personal pecuniary advantage – where the senior officers invariably stood up to shield their colleagues from the vagaries of political expediency. Ghosh did not quite foresee that politicians would in later decades convert politics into the most unregulated, unscrupulous and rewarding of businesses – although the hints were already there.

In recent years, one has seen astounding and disturbing pictures of brazen mass copying in school Board examinations in nearly every examination centre in Bihar, visible to the ordinary eye through every TV channel. Clearly the District Magistrate, Superintendent of Police, District School Inspector, Examination Centre Chief – every authority you can name going right up to the Chief Secretary, Education Minister and Chief Minister – knew exactly what was going on. Would a Menon or TP Singh have permitted mass-copying in school examinations with such impunity? Would they have not have summarily dismissed the DM and District School Inspector for such goings on? Would they not have remonstrated forcefully with their political masters that the most stringent punitive action should be taken and the system revamped to preempt recurrence of such sordid events? Where have the L.P. Singhs, Menons and TP Singhs of yesteryears gone? Have they sold themselves for a handful of silver or a post-retirement sinecure? Have they allowed their discrimination and control of the administrative apparatus to be snatched away and voluntarily abdicated their role to the politicians? Ghosh has made us ponder as to how and why the administration has sunk so low within half-a-century – Bihar is only a reflection of what is happening all over the country.

Ghosh's last assignment was as Chairman of the Tripura Public Service Commission, which he joined after taking voluntary retirement from the IAS. His understated account of direct attempts to influence recruitments to public services and senior level appointments in the state is a forerunner of the rot that afflicts public institutions across the country today, particularly the prevailing venality and self-interest in matters of recruitment and appointment at all levels. An officer who '…had earlier been named for his alleged misdeeds and against whom several vigilance cases were being actively pursued, was appointed on ad hoc basis to a post in the IAS cadre. And this was done brushing aside the recommendation of a statutory selection committee which had removed his name from the select list of officers considered suitable for promotion to the I.A.S. Such extraordinary conduct to reward an officer of dubious integrity confirmed the general belief that he had made some private atonement to the satisfaction of the party in power.' In other words, direct intervention in senior appointments, breaking all conventions and procedures and exposing partisan political interests, had become a reality. Note that Indira Gandhi had already, in the decade of the 1970s, initiated the process of demolishing national institutions. Note also the pernicious practice of Chief Ministers directly involving themselves in mass recruitments to the police forces or for the posts of school teachers, with monetary considerations clearly in mind. This was already evidenced by the end of that decade all over India. The worst damage that can be done to the administration is through venality and corruption in the recruitment systems – in all such cases, the damage that is caused lasts for three decades or so and the blow to the system is enormous. Note also that among the national institutions in Delhi, the Union Public Service Commission is even today one of the very few with an unsullied reputation – and contrast this with the tattered image of nearly every state Public Service Commission in the country. The process clearly started in Tripura, which was then ruled by a communist Chief Minister – a party professing great probity in their politics! Not surprisingly, after the brazen intervention by the government to 'bend' the public service commission, Ghosh 'put in his papers'! This was in 1978.The systemic deterioration of public institutions has galloped apace since then.

There is a reference to the Jai Prakash Narayan movement – alas, too briefly and without throwing much light on the imperatives for the agitation. Most Indians would consider the JP movement as a major event in the nation's history, which highlighted the prevalent state of maladministration, not just in Bihar, but across the country. JP had clearly understood the need for a new political direction, to focus on the needs and aspirations of the common man – and for condemning the general trend among politicians to tend to their own interests at the expense of the citizenry. JP 'sounded his clarion call for pulling down the government, asserting the people's right to disown legislators who had forfeited the right to represent them'. Apparently, the Bihar administration saw the need to put down the JP movement – which they did – much like how the recent Anna Hazare movement was 'handled' by the government of the day.

Ghosh starts his narrative with some hesitation, wondering indeed if he has a story to tell. The story needs telling. He has made a notable contribution to the existing body of administrative literature in India. His is a direct account of what happened in the district and state administration of the country half a century ago.

The story of one significant chunk of India's administrative history has been recounted by Ghosh in an elegant, effective yet uncomplicated style – pleasant to read without being extravagant. The general tenor is understated; there is no use of florid expressions, but his points have been made quietly and tellingly. One can wager that tens of thousands of civil service officers, not just from Bihar but from other parts of India as well, would relive memories of their own years of service through the prism of this chronicle with much nostalgia. Ghosh has made a significant contribution.

Filial Tribute

Abhik Ghosh

Overture

Father completed writing his reminiscences in 1981, clanking away at the old Remington typewriter that belonged to our grandfather. I remember him telling me later that grandfather passed away peacefully on the very day he finished the first draft of his typescript, as though he was waiting for him to finish and did not want to disturb him before it was over.

Disappointed

All of us, his five children, were then preoccupied with our own lives and careers and did not get to see closely what father had written. Much later, he showed me a typewritten copy and asked for my critical comments. To be honest, I was somewhat sceptical at the time as I was not sure if his story would find resonance beyond his immediate circle of family and close friends. He revisited the original draft many times and gave final touches to it in 1992. Thereafter he made several attempts to find an interested publisher, but, somewhere along the way, he gave up.

Retrieved

After his death in 2008, my youngest sister Ketaki retrieved the typescript and wanted to submit it for desktop publication, but somehow that did not happen. At that time, I was posted in Bangkok on an assignment with the International Labour Organization. After my superannuation and return to the country, the thought of somehow fulfilling father's unrealized wishes captured our collective imagination. That is when I got hold of a computer printout of the original typescript and started tinkering around with it.

Vignettes

Father's story as told by him is not an autobiography and does not pretend to be one. It presents vignettes from his experiences as a civil servant, starting from before the country's independence and trudging along into the late 1970s. One reason that encouraged me to undertake the project is that I have actually lived through many of the experiences narrated here and my memory serves me pretty well. Sometimes he would talk to me about them, at other times I would listen in to phone conversations he was wont to have with his contemporaries while sipping his morning cuppa. In many different ways, I was privileged to get a glimpse into his mental and emotional disposition which found expression in variegated shades.

Continuity

The other aspect is that by the time father was ending his career, I was beginning mine. I joined the IAS in 1971 and was allotted the Bihar cadre. Later, I succeeded him in the same office on two occasions, though chronologically separated by a couple of decades: as Managing Director of the Bihar State

Industrial Development Corporation and Commissioner of Tirhut Division. And so, when KW Publishers suggested that it would a fitting tribute if I could also add a concluding chapter to provide a sense of continuity to the narrative, I hesitated at first but soon acquiesced. My siblings also felt that it was a good idea. My sisters contributed by rummaging through old photographs and restoring them to their present condition and youngest brother Amit gave many valuable inputs for my concluding piece.

Jamshedpur Riot

Father's story would remain incomplete without mentioning his significant role in drafting the report of the Jamshedpur Riot Inquiry Commission set up under the Commissions of Inquiry Act. Soon after he returned from his assignment in Tripura and thought he had hung up his boots for good, he was sought out by the Bihar government for appointment as member of a commission to enquire into the communal riots that had wracked Jamshedpur. Justice Jitendra Narain was the titular head and Mr. S.Q. Rizvi from the IPS was the third member. I have seen father labouring over the report, analyzing the root causes of the riot, its immediate provocation and possible conclusions and know that he was pretty much its main architect. It is not without reason that the Jamshedpur report was one of those rare inquiry reports that was accepted by the government in toto and commended as a model of incisive analysis and pragmatic recommendations.

Academia

As I have said earlier, father's reminiscences as a civil servant does not claim to be an all-encompssing autobiography. As such, it is limited in its scope and does not capture all aspects of his many splendoured personality. He was an exceptionally bright student, passing his matriculation in the first division and securing gold medals in both bachelor's and master's degree examinations in History from Patna University. But he also had varied interests in literature, drama, music and other literary and cultural pursuits that kept him preoccupied and somewhat distracted through the academic year and would get down to serious studies only when the examinations were knocking at the door. Soon after completing his master's programme, he followed our grandfather's advice to take a shot at the ICS examination for which an examination centre had started functioning in Delhi. Somewhere midway he abandoned the idea and returned home from Delhi without offering any precise explanation for the volte face. Had he qualified for the ICS in the early 1940s, which I have no doubt he would have, given his consistent academic performance, his story would surely have taken a different turn. Grandfather would privately rue father's decision, which he found somewhat perplexing.

Induction to IAS

As it happened, father was appointed to the provincial civil service by the then British Governor in accordance with the prevailing practice of inducting the best and brightest from the academia into the provincial administration. When he was subsequently promoted to the IAS, he was placed in the 1948 batch. After joining the ILO, I remember telling him in jest that after all I did make it to the ICS, as an international civil servant.

Rare Qualities

His rectitude, his adherence to ethical principles and norms of conduct, his sensitivity, his integrity and honesty of purpose, his reluctance to compromise with mediocrity, his intolerance of perceived injustice – sometimes even his streak of rebelliousness – were qualities that we strove to inculcate.

Although he had an emotional temperament, he would remain remarkably composed when faced with any critical situation and never failed to inspire us with his quiet confidence.

During our growing up years, he hardly ever raised his voice and we cannot recall any instance where he lost his patience with us. Father's approval was of utmost importance to all of us in everything that we did and we invariably looked up to him for his balanced and sagacious counsel. If discipline had to be administered for any reason, he would leave the job entirely to mother, a job she would perform with her characteristic quiet efficiency. When we turned adults, father became more like our friend.

Many Splendoured

Many splendoured he was, without a doubt. Those who knew him well can recall his flair for Bengali and English literature, prose as well as poetry; his love of theatre and music – mostly hindusthani classical and bangla rabindra sangeet; his winsome and gregarious nature; his passion for a brisk game of bridge to unwind after a hard day's work; his partiality for good scotch whisky – blended, not single malt – which he liked to share generously with family and friends. In his twilight years, he would often tell mother how blessed he felt that all their children had imbibed his cherished values and how he was sanguine that we would keep the family traditions burning bright. I cannot judge whether we have proved ourselves worthy of his trust, but such was his generosity. When he felt that his engagement with the outside world was complete, he turned inward and took to kriya yoga of Swami Yogananda. He also devoted much of his time and energies to running the Yogoda Satsanga Mahavidyalaya in Ranchi in close association with the swamis of the Yogoda order. He lived a life fulfilled in every sense and when he left us in 2008 at the age of ninety there was a deep void but no remorse.

Best Years

Like father, I too spent some of my best years as a civil servant in Bihar. I believe the experience both of us gained working as an IAS officer in Bihar was unique in the range of problems and issues we had to deal with on a daily basis. With the kind of grinding we got in our early career, Bihar truly prepared us for assuming progressively higher responsibilities, be they in the state or central government or even in international organizations.

Quid Pro Quo

Like that of my father, my own journey through Bihar was also speckled with skirmishes with politicians of all persuasions and some senior colleagues in the civil service as well. If I were to compare our experiences, there is no doubt that there has been a steady and steep decline in moral and ethical standards leading up to the present. Lamentably, the corruption that is now rampant no longer causes the outrage that it used to as expediency has become the name of the game. Most of those who claim to govern the state on the basis of a democratic mandate, which is quite often rigged, far too easily become pompous, self-serving and downright dishonest. And then they look out for civil servants who are only too willing to oblige them in their quest for power and pelf. Quite often it turns into a game of quid pro quo, with pliant and 'committed' civil servants swearing allegiance to transient political masters in return for untimely and undeserved rewards.

The Long Shadow

A notable feature of Bihar's socio-political architecture is the acute awareness of individual identities, belief systems and caste loyalties, which inevitably gets reflected in its faction-ridden politics and statecraft. I hasten to add that the scourge is not confined to Bihar, as revealed by recent unprincipled electoral alliances in some southern states. The identity politics currently in play in the heartland of Uttar Pradesh in the run-up to the state elections of 2017 provide further evidence that caste and religion will continue to remain strong forces in all manner of political alignments in the foreseeable future.

Regretfully, in pursuing the numbers game, we have made little progress in the direction of reconciling and unifying the contentious groups in our society, which is the real foundation of nationality. One would have thought that economic development, the spread of education, migrations to other states and the national capital region and such other levelling influences would curb the insidious role of caste in politics, but recent events in Bihar have cast a long shadow of doubt. In his first term, Chief Minister Nitish Kumar was hailed as Vikas Purush and Susashan Babu – mascot of development and good governance. But, when push came to shove, his alliance with the RJD for the 2015 state assembly elections appears to have been motivated mainly by the compulsions of the caste and communal arithmetic.

Good Governance?

To be sure, many good things happened during Nitish Kumar's first term as Chief Minister: law and order was markedly improved; roads were built; primary education and rural health programmes received a lot of attention; power supply was decidedly enhanced. In general, the political stock of Bihar soared and there was a palpable sense of pride among those who belonged to the state. But after Nitish chose to chart his own course, opting for RJD as his electoral partner, doubts and apprehensions have begun raising their heads. Questions are being asked whether all his assurances of good governance will actually endure. There is already some talk about Bihar's return to jungle raj, which is how Laloo Yadav's years as Chief Minister is often described. History will ultimately judge whether the JDU-RJD alliance was a marriage of sheer convenience to satisfy personal and dynastic ambitions of the present lot of political leaders or whether it served the public good and larger interests of the state. The jury is still out on this.

Hope Springs Eternal

There is light at the end of the tunnel. Perhaps. It will require a leader of exceptional qualities – a great integrator with proven navigational skills – to steer the ship of state, avoid the whirlpools, and restore Bihar's pristine glory. The good news is that there are still many among our tribe of upright civil servants and an emerging genre of young, well educated and well intentioned politicians who can rise above the temptations of their immediate surroundings and carry the torch. For the incurable optimist, hope springs eternal.

A familiar sight: morning tea in the garden

In front of District Magistrate's Bungalow, Munger

On the lawns of Commissioner's House, Muzaffarpur

Prologue

I owe an explanation for inflicting on the reader yet another of those reminiscences of a retired civil servant. Many distinguished administrators who held centre stage in their life and times have set down their rare experiences, letting in the reader to little-known facts that were both interesting and edifying. The stories they narrate relate mostly to mega events or major dramatis personae at the national level. The little things that happen every now and then in the dimly lit corners of our states that have quietly shaped the personality and character of our administration and the fate of our peoples have rarely found mention in such narratives. The experiences of a middle-level civil servant who came in close contact with some of those small yet significant events should, I assume, help reach a better understanding of how and why we have arrived at our present state of affairs in our affairs of state.

The locale here is confined to a state with which the appellation 'backward' has stuck for many years. Despite all its hidden mineral wealth underground, its plentiful rainfall and fertile soil, and its populace of sturdy and honest folks, Bihar has stood out as the epitome of all that has gone wrong with our polity. Having witnessed here scenes of high hope and abysmal frustration, I felt that perhaps I had something to share with a wider audience. The discerning reader will not fail to recognize that many of the events narrated here were harbingers of later developments unfolding on the national stage.

I have said a good deal about politicians and their power play. In doing so, I have been acutely conscious of my limitations to be able to speak with authority on the subject. My observations may, however, provide an insider view of the moves of state level politicians in their quest for power, which soon reached a stage where these desperate men freely staked the interests of the state for their partisan political ends.

All this was but incidental. Having retired from active service, I initially sat myself down to recapitulate my experiences with a feeling of nostalgia, hoping to be able to give to my readers a flavour of our times. As I went along I noticed that my narrative was losing its original plot as memories of events unfolded relentlessly, with parallels that could be drawn with scenarios that have become only too familiar today. The reason I did not give up my enterprise was because I found in those early events some tones of what has become today's dominant ethos.

My friend Aswini Kumar Chattoraj was the one who provoked me into undertaking this uncharted course of reciting the annals of our times spent in the Bihar administration. Aswini retired as a Deputy Collector after having worked for many years as Personal Assistant to Dr. Shri Krishna Sinha, the first Chief Minister, who guided Bihar's destiny for more than a decade and half. Not only did Aswini egg me on to undertake this hazardous journey, he also shared with me some little- known episodes to which he was privy. I completed the narrative way back in 1981 and let it lie over, after toying for some time with the idea of publishing it in some form for wider circulation. I was persuaded to revive the idea by my friend Dr. Pijushendu Gupta, former Editor of the Behar Herald, who convinced me that the story of our times – mundane as it may appear at first sight – needed telling. I agreed with him mainly because not much has really been written about how, after all the sacrifices that our political leaders made during the struggle for freedom from British rule, their basal weaknesses got the better of them as the powers and spoils of office inevitably took hold.

This manuscript may not have not have seen the light of day without the encouragement and assistance of Dr. Gupta and the zeal of Sri Gautam Roy, Secretary, Bihar Writers' Press Cooperative Society. There were several others who contributed to this tome with their critical appraisal and comments. I am grateful to all my friends and well-wishers, only a few of whom I have named.

Ranchi, 15th August 1992 **S.K. Ghosh**

Initiation and Some Foretastes

On 28th April 1942, I stepped into the residential office of Mr. W.G. Archer, I.C.S., District Magistrate and Collector of Patna, presenting myself as the new Deputy Collector who had joined the previous day. This was my first acquaintance with the British ruler in action at his post. I had left college less than two years ago. The intervening period – spent in preparing for competitive examinations for entry into one of the All India or Central Services (recruitment to the services in Bihar was not made through competitive examinations in those days) – had helped me retain some of the uninhibited outlook of a University student. While still at college, I had seen big-wigs of the Indian Civil Service sit through college functions, looking quite ordinary in that setting. I recollect how I had enjoyed one of them being worsted in a debate with Dr. Gyan Chand, our Professor of Economics in Patna College, while attempting to find flaws in some radical economic theories that the good professor had expounded. To see a Britisher thus outwitted was indeed an experience to store up.

In keeping with the general attitude of irreverence which had grown in me as a free-thinking student of those days, I felt none of the awe which one commonly associated with facing the majesty of the British 'Raj' symbolised by the Collector and District Magistrate. I was, in fact, amused by the manner in which Mr. Archer sought to size me up. As I walked in, I noticed that he had pulled his chair some distance away from the centre of his office table, thus creating more viewing space across which he intently watched every approaching step of mine. I felt something of a human touch in his whole demeanour. As I came to know later, Mr. Archer possessed an academic bent of mind, was intensely interested in social anthropology and also was quite unorthodox for a British civilian of his time. Not only did he make friends with middle class Indian families, he even stayed in their homes on occasion. My first introduction to the official world was thus rather pleasant.

I was to learn soon that Mr. Archer would rarely be seen or his presence felt by junior officers like us. He applied himself wholeheartedly to work connected with the "war effort" – the Second World War was not going too well for the Allied powers – leaving the routine administration in the care of a seasoned Deputy Collector, who had been promoted as Additional District Magistrate.

Khan Bahadur A.N.M. Omar, Additional District Magistrate of Patna, took immediate charge of me and lost no time to start breaking me in. The first round in the process began with his asking me to attend his residential office every day at half past four in the afternoon to assist him in sifting through the 'dak'. This was summer time in Bihar when public offices and courts worked only in the morning hours. So, returning home for lunch some time past mid-day, I had to pick up my bicycle again by quarter past four in the afternoon to pedal through a distance of about four kilometers, with the afternoon sun still blazing, to arrive on time for my daily chore.

The Collector's 'dak' is a huge pile of assorted communications addressed formally to the head of the district administration. Much of the mail consists of notices, summons, papers and records in transmission and only a few of them were truly meant for his eyes and which he had to attend to at once. If the real stuff was missed at the initial stage, it would get suppressed in the pile of correspondence and pushed down the chute. It would then be "diarised", 'docketed', processed and eventually put up in the file 'for orders', having passed through half-a-dozen intermediaries in the process.

Perched on a chair, which someone had thoughtfully placed alongside a table on the open verandah of the Additional District Magistrate's residence, I went through the rather mechanical process of scanning the mail without getting any the wiser about the significance of this daily chore. After all the correspondence had been neatly stacked, the Khan Bahadur would come out in his own time to take up the serious business of initialing the 'dak'. A minor clerk stood keyed up by the edge of the table and, no sooner had the page at the top of the pile taken the boss's initials, the clerk would flick it away to offer the next one for a similar treatment. Thanks to this training, I was later able to take a functional, rather than a mechanical, approach to sorting and sifting through the 'dak' and removing the grain from the chaff.

No sooner had I embarked on my training in receiving and readying the daily mail, I got a tug on the reins on the first Sunday that followed. Something prompted me to mention to my mentor that I would absent myself from work on the ensuing Sunday. I was told gently, but in unequivocal terms, that I could take time off if I had some personal business to attend to, but not just because it happened to be a Sunday. This was indeed a telling assertion that the services of a whole-time government servant were at the disposal of the government at all hours of the day and night, every day of the week.

On one of those evenings during my early grooming, I noticed a dapper young man walking up the steps of the verandah with a sparkle in his eyes and a complexion as fresh as dew. The Khan Bahadur was all smiles, greeting him at the threshold. Being close to the 'place of occurrence', I was called in and introduced. This was the first of my several meetings with S.V. Sohoni, I.C.S. who was then an Under Secretary to the government. I soon discovered that the Khan Bahadur had invited him for afternoon tea. He called me in to join them without, of course, letting it appear as an invitation. This was perhaps another lesson which my mentor wanted to impart – that a junior officer of the provincial service was really a non-entity and could be taken for granted. I forgot the lesson – but not my mentor – for this practical demonstration of how condescending a superior officer of the service could be.

I did not have to hang around the Khan Bahadur for long. With the outbreak of civil disturbances in August 1942, the routine was broken and he was transferred out soon thereafter. I cannot, however, end the story of my early experiences as a probationary officer without recounting one more lesson I received from my mentor. The government wanted a report about the Anglo-Burmese refugees who had moved into Patna in large numbers. The Additional District Magistrate gave me the task of preparing a report. I moved around the town, met the refugees individually, and prepared a fairly comprehensive report within a couple of days. When I presented it to my boss, there was not a word of appreciation. I was only privileged to witness the art of appropriation. The Khan Bahadur took my report and, with his usual flair, added a preamble and a conclusion, filling them with some verbal roughage. He then affixed his flowing signature at the end, thereby deftly effacing the report's real author and sent it off verbatim to the government. The Khan Bahadur, may his soul rest in peace, was obviously imparting another lesson in self-effacement, particularly in the presence of superior officers.

By now almost a year had elapsed and it was assumed that I had learnt whatever there was to learn, although I had not yet become acquainted with, nor received, any practical training in revenue law and administration, civil laws and procedures and trial of criminal cases. The days of Administrative Training Institutes were far away, where probationers are left to browse in the libraries or listen to erudite lectures from subject matter specialists, much like University students, with a view to sharpening their minds in preparation for the departmental examinations to be taken at the conclusion of their training. My representation to the government for condoning the delay in completing my departmental examinations, on the unassailable ground that I was employed on special assignments throughout my probation period and did not get time off to prepare for them, was summarily rejected.

Within a year of my joining the service, I was assigned to deal with a task that was completely new for the administration of the day, namely price control and civil supplies. The problems were unique and there was little by way of guidance. Procurement and storage of food grains on a large scale and regulation of markets were completely new challenges. It led eventually to the introduction of some form of rationing, beginning with the capital city of Patna. All these tasks became a major operation by the early summer of 1943. They were in fact considered an integral part of the 'war effort', so much so that when the Viceroy Lord Wavell paid a visit to Patna one of his principal engagements was to inspect food grain godowns and ration shops, which took him to congested market areas situated in the narrow lanes and by lanes of Bakergunj in Patna.

Beginning with taking delivery of railway wagons loaded with food grains, weighing the bags and storing them in improvised godowns — the Golghar of Patna was converted into one— I soon graduated to the post of Price Control Officer, and later, Assistant Rationing Officer, exercising statutory powers under the Defence of India Rules. By the end of 1943, the entire district was covered by a system of rationing and a full time Additional District Magistrate was appointed to handle the job. This was how I came to be placed under another veteran of the provincial civil service, Mr. P.N. Mazumdar, who was already a Rai Sahib and would soon be decorated as Rai Bahadur. Mr. Mazumdar was a man of impeccable character; only, he did not like the idea of anyone getting some fun out of life. He grudged my taking a short leave for my honeymoon for which I had secured prior permission from the Collector just before Mr. Mazumdar took up his post. Though not brilliant by any standard, his unimpeachable integrity was the solid foundation on which the rationing system of Patna was successfully built. Mr. Mazumdar made me squarely responsible for whatever was needed to be done to make the rationing system work seamlessly and it was largely due to the unreserved trust he reposed in me that within a short period of time I came of age.

Soon I was given full charge of rationing of cloth. The Additional District Magistrate in charge of Rationing had by then been replaced by a Special Officer, who exercised only nominal control over rationing of cloth. It was in this assignment that I was thrown among the wolves, as it were. There were the big 'importers' receiving consignments directly from the cloth mills and stashing some of them away, the wholesalers fudging accounts to take out bales of cloth to feed the 'black' market or occasionally faking big thefts in their stores to divert their stocks, the ubiquitous politicians demanding special favours, in a low key to begin with —and getting ever more strident, the influential socialites looking for fine and extra-fine textiles beyond the rationed quotas. Top level civil servants, up to the rank of Secretaries to the government, conducted periodic reviews of the programme, which as a mere probationer I was privileged to attend. I can never forget how they invariably protected me from allegations of overbearing conduct on my part.

One such incident bears narration. Mr. Gordon was the Resident Engineer of the Patna Electric Supply Company, which was a British-owned concern. His extremely comely wife descended on my office one morning and asked for a special quota of cloth for distribution among 'her workers'. Government orders on the subject of supply of cloth to organized labour through their Trade Unions were explicit and unambiguous and I had no option but to resist Mrs. Gordon's high-minded proposal, notwithstanding her charming personality. I tried my very best to explain why I could not be of any use to her, but from her demeanour it was evident that she was not satisfied with my explanations, being the kind of woman who was not accustomed to taking 'no' for an answer. Complaints about my rude behaviour with the lady reached the Adviser to the Governor and clarifications were sought. But, to the credit of norms established by the British Raj, nothing about the episode was conveyed to me in writing. The Collector once asked me what the fracas was all about and I was called to meet the Cloth Controller to whom I narrated what had transpired. That was the end of the matter. Later, when I was once in the presence of Mr. K.S.V. Raman, I.C.S., then Secretary in the Supply Department, he asked me if I was the fellow who had refused to oblige the implacable lady. He then gave me one of his unforgettable grins, which was like a hundred pats on my back.

With the formation of the interim government at the Centre, a Congress government headed by Dr. Shri Krishna

Sinha was inducted in Bihar in 1946. One of its first tasks was to popularize the administration of civil supplies, which resulted in setting up committees with nominated non-officials. Very soon, I found myself in trouble again.

Despite my cordial relations with most of the committee members – Babu Jagjiwan Ram headed one of them for a while – the combination of forces proved strong enough to cause me much harassment and humiliation. I had, of course, given cause for annoyance to the non-official committee members by failing to respond to their private demands. During one such committee meeting a disgruntled member called into question some action I had taken, describing it as 'shilly shallying'. When I challenged him with facts that were plainly incontrovertible and exposed his deliberate attempts at distortion, sharp came a retort form his ally that between two versions, one from a mere official and the other from a non-official, the latter must prevail. I was stunned at the sheer audacity of such a brash conclusion, but not a word was uttered to soften its harshness. One of my non-official friends in the committee, the late Zaffar Imam who become a minister many years later, whispered in my ear not to take such matters to heart. They were inherent in the democratic ways of functioning, he confided.

The second phase of my orientation concluded not long thereafter with my developing duodenal ulcer and proceeding on long leave in March 1947. As a foretaste of things to come, the person chosen to fill the post vacated by me was a briefless lawyer, past his middle age, whose one strong point was his penchant for astrology, with which he placated politicians in positions of influence. His was an 'ad hoc' appointment for a limited period, which did not require the concurrence of the Public Service Commission.

Independence and Some Early Trends

Independence came in August, 1947. The sheer ecstasy, never to be tasted again, sought expression in public and private celebrations, but they could hardly match the intensity of our innermost feelings, however high we may have been in 'spirits'. I had recently joined as a Deputy Collector at Ranchi and, as a part of the official programme of celebrations for the ensuing event, I was sent out to meet the simple tribals of neighbouring rural areas to tell them what independence was all about. When I addressed the crowds gathered at the village hatias I found that I was making little impression, not because of the inadequacy of my language skills, but because of the strangeness of the concept and its sheer abstraction. My exhortations to the tribals to celebrate the event in a befitting manner produced but one lone voice from the assembly, pleading for release of a special quota of kerosene oil which was in short supply. With some show of enthusiasm, I carried back the idea to my Sub-divisional Officer who just laughed it off, saying something to the effect that the common villager did not need kerosene oil for lighting his little earthen lamp. The poor tribal would obtain the priceless gift of freedom, which we were encouraging him to celebrate, but I was left wondering how he would fulfill his dream of lighting up his own home?

Early in the forenoon of 15th August 1947, with telltale marks of late night celebrations showing on many of our faces, the officers of the district assembled in the Deputy Commissioner's chamber to take a new oath of allegiance to the country and its people. Our hearts were full and hopes rose sky-high. Cries of agony that rent the air of north India on either side of the line of partition in the Punjab and the muffled groans of refugees trekking from the eastern part of what was united Bengal were lost in the elation of the hour, far removed as we were in Bihar from the scenes of those cataclysmic events.

The first Congress government in Bihar in free India was headed by Dr. Shri Krishna Sinha who had earlier led the provincial government under the Government of India Act from 1937-39 and, again later, during the short-lived interim government preceding the transfer of power. Dr. Sinha was a man of great vision and was endowed with a large heart. He was also intensely human, possessing an emotional nature and subject as much to its frailties. An avid reader, his personal collection of books now adorns the library of the Shri Krishna Seva Sadan at Munger, the headquarter town of the district from which he hailed. The courage he displayed in fighting for the cause of independence had earned him the sobriquet of 'Bihar Keshari", the lion of Bihar. A compelling orator to top it all, he was the undisputed leader of Bihar. He had a close ally and comrade in Anugraha Narain Sinha, an astute politician and pragmatic administrator with a sharp mind.

His winsome ways earned for him friends from all sections of society and he reciprocated their friendships with characteristic generosity. Anugraha Babu's influence was next only to that of Dr. Shri Krishna Sinha. Among others in the Government were Pandit Binodananda Jha, a Brahmin from one of the principal Panda families of Deoghar; Sri Jaglal Choudhary, a member of the scheduled castes; Dr. Syed Mahmud, a senior leader of nationalist Muslims; and Mr. Krishna Ballabh Sahay, a Kayastha from the district of Hazaribagh. I have deliberately avoided mentioning the castes of the two top Sinhas because, quite clearly, their stature at the time transcended all caste affiliations. The other Ministers were also chosen on their individual merits and not only for their caste followings. But, even in those early days at the dawn of independence, caste factors had to be recognized as an indispensible element in government formation. It did not take us long to discover the depths to which the roots of caste loyalties had penetrated the soil of Bihar. For the administrator, assessment of any situation would be incomplete unless it had taken into account the hidden "caste factor".

Back in the early days of the first Congress government of free India, we soon began witnessing scenes of high enthusiasm interspersed with high drama. Ministers thought nothing of chastising officers in full public view on hearing one-sided versions of acts of omission and commission on their part. Indeed, they seemed to derive a strange satisfaction by conducting themselves publicly in this manner, as if to demonstrate that almost overnight they had brought about a real change in the style of governance, freeing it from the unhealthy legacies of the past and making it truly responsive and responsible to the people. One Minister played the legendary Harun-Al-Rashid, visiting police stations incognito, mercifully without applying any cosmetic product to disguise his visage and not needing one either. Appearing as a poor villager of lowly status, he would narrate tales of wrongdoing and harassment at the hands of some bigwigs and seek the assistance of the local police. Often he would be brusquely turned away, whereupon he would reveal his identity and bring the unsuspecting police officer down on his knees. Dr. Shri Krishna Sinha, emotional as he was, initially fell for a similar temptation and dealt with some errant officers abruptly on one or two occasions. But, very soon he realized the unfairness and deleterious effects of such dramatic acts and adopted the more dignified practice of holding free and frank talks with officers against whom public complaints were received.

Placing the blame on officers for unsatisfactory performance of government programmes soon became the pet grouse of politicians. So much so that when field officials were called upon to engage with local residents and obtain their support in programme implementation, they would often fight shy of programmes that might jeopardize the vested interests of locally influential politicians.

Early in 1948, the government sanctioned a programme for renovation, repair and fresh construction of minor irrigation works that the local landlords had neglected to maintain, notwithstanding their legal obligations to do so. The abolition of the 'zamindari' system was imminent. The main objective of the programme was to provide water for irrigating the fields during the cyclical bouts of drought, but it was also meant to demonstrate the government's resolve to deliver the 'raiyat' from the age-old system of exploitation by the zamindars. Unfortunately, the government's sanction for the project was conveyed only six weeks or so before the end of the fiscal year, beyond which the fund allocations would lapse. Huge funds were practically forced upon the field officers and they were expected to deliver on time. I was then posted as Additional S.D.O. (Revenue), with jurisdiction over two sub-divisions of the undivided Ranchi district — Gumla and Simdega. The area within my charge, which later constituted a separate district, was spread over about 4,000 sq km in hilly terrain. Within the short time available, I was required to select and get a large number of minor irrigation schemes executed in the hills and valleys. Technical support at the field level was virtually non-existent and there was nothing like the infrastructure set up later under the Community Development Programme. In these circumstances our task, as a colleague of mine with a flair for homely imagery put it, was like trying to fetch milk from a bird's nest.

On one of my several desperate searches for locating a suitable site for a minor irrigation bundh, I drove my old Chevvy into the deep ruts of a cart track that broke her wheel bearings. Fortunately, the local sponsor of the scheme was accompanying me and helped me pull out and drive the car back onto one side of the highway. By then evening had descended, and I was not feeling too inclined to push on for the rest of the 25 km to my headquarters. My companion walked up to a nearby house of a tribal villager and asked him if he could take in a guest for the night. Yes, I was welcome and, soon enough, after a refreshing wash in the cool waters of the well, I spread my bed roll on a 'charpoi' pulled out under a pleasant starry summer night. The master of the house, a man of few words, put me in the care of his teen-aged daughter, who was a student of the local mission school and was the only other member of the household. While her father got busy cooking a meal for us and I stretched my limbs on the bed, my little friend prattled on about her school and her books. I was completely rested and ravenously hungry when dinner was announced. My host offered me a simple fare of rice and dal, with bits of green mango thrown in to turn it into a delicacy. I cannot recall a more satisfying meal and a more restful sleep that followed.

In no time, the local party bosses became critical of our style of functioning. They were not being fully associated with the programme, they complained, even though they themselves took no initiative to visit the hot and dusty villages to identify sites for the irrigation schemes. They also complained that we were entertaining suggestions from the Christian missionaries. But they were the ones who knew the area well and worked in the most inaccessible and remote corners. There was, of course, a political angle to it. The ruling party was looking for a foothold amongst the tribals— who had to be weaned away from the influence of the missionaries. But the party workers were only interested in the politics and had little to offer by way of service.

This somewhat lengthy narration of how a particular programme was implemented has been necessary, not only because it was the first to be taken up on an extensive scale and contained immense potential for public good, but also because it showed up the weaknesses from which our development programmes have suffered throughout. Its characteristic features have been the hasty conception of projects— compounded by inadequate planning, failure to garner organizational resources, indecent rush and, above all, lack of motivation and consequent failure to enthuse the intended beneficiaries. Over the years, far from learning from past experiences, our political masters appear to have given up even the pretence of delivering real development, looking instead for gimmicks that would earn them quick publicity, often with something extra that could take care of the rainy days.

My First Sub-division: A Package Deal

In February 1949, I was transferred to Giridih, then only a sub-divisional headquarter, to function as the 'second officer', the official next below the Sub-divisional Magistrate. It was here that my wife set up our first home, but only after some waiting in search of a suitable house. Times have now changed, but in those years it was still a tradition with local inhabitants to reach out and help officers coming to stay in their midst. Just when I was feeling literally sick of staying on in the cramped dak bungalow, we were offered temporary accommodation in a house owned by a gentleman from Calcutta, who retained it for occasional week-end visits. The caretaker hoped we would not get in his way and allowed us stay there for a fortnight. It was a neat, well-appointed house with a manicured lawn and we lost no time in moving in and spreading out over the entire ground floor to make the most of our good fortune. We had barely spent three days in expansive comfort when, late one evening, as we were having dinner in the brightly illuminated dining room, a car carrying a portly gentleman drove in. When I went out to meet him I noticed the look of bewilderment on his face. After a short pause, he introduced himself as the owner of the house. When I tried to explain my presence, he laughed softly and invited me to make myself comfortable until I had found a suitable accommodation elsewhere. My search took me to Mrs. Bose of B.B. Cottage.

I had been forewarned by my colleagues that I should be prepared to take a refusal, for Mrs. Bose was a formidable landlady who apparently was not too keen to take on local officers as her tenants. It was now my turn to be surprised. Mrs. Bose accepted me with a big grin and assured me that the house would be made ready for us within a couple of days. And throughout our stay in Giridih, Mrs. Bose looked after us like a commiserating aunt, and memories of our first real home were indelibly etched on our minds. My posting in Giridih, however, turned out to be a quick preparation for a full sub-divisional charge. In less than nine months, I moved for my first posting as Sub-divisional Officer in the Sadar sub-division of Darbhanga.

Darbhanga, the home of the Maithils, was the most densely populated district of Bihar before its reorganization and has remained a difficult charge at all levels and in the best of times. Apart from the plethora of problems besetting the district, the complex character of Maithils is believed to be a contributory factor. The Maithils have a cultural history which few other communities can equal. But, successive natural calamities, floods followed by periodic droughts, coupled with social atrophy caused by the declining importance of Sanskrit studies, had left the Maithilis with little more than memories of their glorious past. Fallen as they had from grace, the minds that wove the finest of poetry, unwound the knotty intricacies of 'nyaya' and practiced the esoteric Tantric cult, found the deprivations of an impoverished economy more degrading than others who did not share their history. The very sophistication of the Maithils made them highly complex individuals to deal with, particularly for civil servants who, as a class, were not ordinarily endowed with empathy and understanding.

I may have been hasty in observing earlier that I had graduated as a civil servant. My experiences in Darbhanga truly initiated me into the intricacies of my life ahead. Short of conducting a general election, there was not a single task or situation that I did not have to deal with here that other generalist administrators would take years to encounter at different stages of their career. The package deal turned out to be a trial by fire.

Flood relief operations had ended in my sub-division barely six weeks before I joined and the air was thick with complaints of administrative lapses. The business of relief was something I was not familiar with. So, within days of my joining I went around the flood-stricken areas, in course of which I also spent one night on a wooden bench in the abandoned dak-bungalow of village Rasiari. The name reminded me of 'Rasia', the lover-god of Vidyapati's poems. I reached Rasiari after crossing village Ghanshyampur, which literally means the abode of the dark blue-green, once again bringing back to me the tales of the playful Krishna. Despite these evocative names, the flood-affected plains were stark, barren and devastated.

Having seen at close quarters the hungry looks of flood-stricken men and women and resolving to do better, I applied myself to the judicial work that was my mainstay. The sub-divisional magistrate's 'General File', with some half a dozen complaint cases and quite as many proceedings under various sections of the Criminal Procedure Code, a number of bail applications and several cases for trial to boot, put me to the severest test. I soon learnt to pronounce expeditious judicial decisions, without committing obvious errors of fact and law.

Despite the heavy judicial work requiring the application of an undisturbed mind, exciting things kept happening elsewhere within my jurisdiction that demanded my immediate attention. The crops were now ready for harvesting and, in the dominantly feudal structure of Darbhanga society, disputes over lands and their produce — mainly between the substantial landholders and their subordinate tenants, mostly share-croppers — broke out like a seasonal rash. No sooner was this contained, the dry summer brought in its wake an epidemic of 'village' fires. A spark flying from an open stove and catching the dry thatched roofs burnt entire villages, requiring the organization of immediate relief and rehabilitation for the victims. In between, there would be incidents which, if not promptly tackled, might have escalated into major communal clashes.

As if these were not enough, a severe drought overtook Darbhanga and, indeed, much of Bihar in 1950. This required advance planning for finding employment and food for people who derived sustenance mainly from agriculture, the period of drought extending from the winter of that year until the next rainy season. After a quick survey, I drew up the basics of a scheme for launching immediate relief operations and sent my proposals to the Collector, Mr. U.K. Ghosh. The Collector was a hard task-master and a relentless worker himself, with a weakness for creating work where none existed. To my pleasant surprise, he wrote effusive comments on my proposal and desired that it should be shown to my colleagues in the other two sub-divisions, apparently as a model for similar action. My colleagues must have viewed the whole thing just as one more item of avoidable work created by the Collector.

Notwithstanding the prevailing drought, the floods arrived dutifully on their annual visitation. Besides providing medical facilities for rough-and-ready treatment of ailments and accidents associated with water-bound conditions, mobilizing boats and boatmen to keep up the supply of essential commodities, the main aspect of the flood-relief programme was distribution of doles to the indigent population. The working men naturally moved out elsewhere in search of employment. Those who stayed behind, other than the indigent, were the ones who need not or would not work for a living and, having nothing better to do - not even the free exercise of their muscles to use up their unspent energy - engaged themselves in fierce gossip centred around the only visible activity, which was the relief operation.

Having already resolved to do better, I brought about some reorientation in the administration of flood relief by informally associating local Congress party workers who were willing to help identify the real indigent populations by a village-by-village survey, after which they would be provided with identity cards for receiving the doles. The doles would be distributed by the Zonal Relief Officers, who would be accompanied by party workers on their visits to the interior villages. I got the dole vouchers issued as bound books in which the counterfoils would be retained, to be able to verify later that the doles had indeed been received by the needy and indigent.

What proved to be the Achilles' heel of this new strategy was the association of public workers, for it turned out that the ones active in the area were led by a person belonging to one of the two factions within the district Congress party. The powers of office had already begun casting their spell and ruling party workers were getting aligned with prominent patrons. In Darbhanga, one group was led by the President of the district unit of the party and the other by the Chairman of the District Board. The leader of the first group was a trusted lieutenant of Sri Anugraha Narain Sinha.

The latter group felt alienated from the relief operations due to its own inaction. It chose, therefore, to send petitions to the Collector alleging gross abuse of relief materials and other resources. Mr. U.K. Ghosh sent the District Kosi Relief Officer for an enquiry, not bothering to advise me about it in advance. The officer indirectly supported the allegations by commenting that the Zonal Relief Officers had come under the sway of the leader of one of the warring factions. His report was then forwarded to me for comments. Mr. U.K. Ghosh, the man of action that he was, wanted me to review everything personally and remove all blemishes forthwith. The receding floods made travel by boat impractical and so I planned a realistic expedition.

The first part of the journey was accomplished by train, going up to Jhanjharpur some 30 km away, where I reached late in the evening. Unrolling my bed on the deck of the waiting bullock cart, I stretched myself for the overnight journey ahead. With plaintive notes emanating from the wheels of the bullock cart and regular beats keeping time whenever the springless cart hit a myriad potholes, I fell into blissful 'yogic' slumber. On awakening, the sight that greeted me was also truly a 'yogi's' prerogative. The scarlet rays of dawn were streaming through an opening in the hood covering the front of the cart. Ghanshyampur appeared before me bathed in the shimmering light of dawn. True to its name, it was lush green in portions that had escaped the fury of the floods. Beyond the turbid waters on its fringes and silhouetted in soft golden light lurked village Rasiari. Roused, I crossed the water body in a boat and pitched my tent on top of a thatch roof that stuck out from the water spread all around.

We drew up a plan to leave immediately and travel from village to village during the rest of the day and the following two days to verify the complaints locally. But, as boats and bullock carts could not negotiate the swamps left behind by the receding floods, we chose the amphibious elephant as our beast of burden. The sight of a caparisoned elephant moving in a procession or carrying laughing children on its back in a zoological park leaves a highly deceptive idea of what riding on elephant back over long distances can be like. As the elephant moved, its rippling muscles felt like waves rising and falling on its back, with the rider helplessly clutching on for dear life. After the day's ride for over 10 km, I felt I could do with a new set of muscles. Thanks to the nightly massages,

I lived through the ordeal of the next two days and returned with my original frame intact.

The enquiry proved to be a great disappointment for those who had raised a hue and cry. Thanks to the new system of 'book keeping', we could verify on the spot, that every payment had been correctly made to the genuinely indigent beneficiaries and had been duly accounted for. Frustration in the ranks of the complainants soon vented in a scuffle between the two rival groups. It was the last day of the enquiry and I had already climbed atop the elephant's back, ready to leave for my camp. As my admonitions to the warring groups to cease squabbling did not have any impact, I jumped straight into the melee. The dramatic drop spread enough confusion to scatter the crowd. That was the dramatic end to the complaints against me of 'abuse' of relief supplies.

The lesson imprinted on my mind would serve me for the rest of my career. I had committed the folly of inviting participation of willing party workers in implementing the flood relief programme, without adequately balancing the factional elements— although it was already becoming amply clear that attempts to neutralise the contending factions may not have yielded the desired results.

I did not miss the experience of a communal situation in the omnibus package that was Darbhanga. Barely within nine months of my stay, a communal riot broke out in Nari-Bhadaon village in Biraul police station. Before the riot could gather momentum, the officer-in-charge had arrived on the scene and managed to contain it. I camped in the village for nearly a week, pitching my tent in an open field, and finally saw the two communities joining hands and re-building the burnt houses.

The conduct of some men during my stay in the affected village warned me, however, to be watchful of possible repercussions during the ensuing Bakr-Id festival. Disputes over cow slaughter during Bakr-Id used to be live issues in those days, capable of triggering communal clashes. The confrontations occurred mostly in the rural areas that were often not easily accessible. And, in our days there was one, yes just one, jeep at the Darbhanga district headquarters for use by all touring officers stationed there. With the experience gathered during my stay at Nari-Bhadaon, I took the officer-in-charge of Biraul police station into confidence and drew up a contingency plan. In the upshot, the leaders among potential mischief-makers along with some of their associates were bound down under Section 107 of the Criminal Procedure Code and kept behind bars on the eve of Bakr-Id.

Recalling the poor mobility and lack of resources in our days, one is tempted to ask whether today's vastly improved facilities have brought an unmixed blessing for good governance. The speed with which an officer can reach the remotest areas under his charge is undoubtedly of great advantage and, in today's conditions, it would be foolhardy to think of managing without the essential facilities and infrastructure. But, despite the many time-saving devices, one wonders how many still find the time to stay in the midst of villagers, partake of their simple fare and empathise with their bare living conditions. I recall the words of Bradford Spangenberg who, writing about the quality of district administration in the latter part of the 19th century, said: "as officials became more sophisticated in their technological professionalization, the less they knew or were forced to know about the people". Spangenburg said this in the context of the spread of the telegraph network in India.

The impluses of the new order did not escape Darbhanga for long. The first legal battle over implementation of the law for acquisition of intermediary interests in land was fought in the court of the subordinate judge of Darbhanga, where the Maharajadhiraj had filed a suit challenging its validity. Victory in the first round was his, but the Raja knew his days were numbered and conducted himself throughout with traditional dignity and grace. What seemed to hurt the members of the 'royal' household most was the loss of their primacy vis-à-vis the local administration, a 'privilege' they had long enjoyed. So, when in breach of established protocol, Mr. U.K. Ghosh failed to call on the Maharajadhiraj or his brother the Raja Bahadur on assuming charge of the district, they felt cut to the quick. The Maharajidhiraj mostly lived outside Darbhanga. But his younger brother, Raja Bahadur, the doyen of Darbhanga's social elite, nursed the slight and was on the lookout for an opportunity to settle the score. With their common interest in 'shikar', the Raja Bahadur had struck a friendship with the Divisional Commissioner Mr. H. Lal. He now invited Mr. Lal to stay at his Bela Palace during one of his official visits to Darbhanga. Mr. Lal was "willin' and happy" to please his royal host and Raja Bahadur had the satisfaction of seeing the Collector come running to his palace where his boss was camping.

The winds of change were blowing hard and fast. Some time after I had left Darbhanga, in the first general election to the Lok Sabha in 1951, the Maharajadhiraj was challenged in his own territory by a Congressman who was a political lightweight at the time. The victor was Mr. Shyam Nandan Mishra, who was much later appointed as Minister for External Affairs in the short-lived Charan Singh government.

To conclude the story of my highly instructive and eventful term as a Sub-divisional Officer—after I left Darbhanga a tale was carried through the town about my having knocked at the door of a 'Women's Home' late one night. There was another tale – which hopefully was not a mere tale – that I was one officer who could be frequently found mingling with the common folks in the countryside, listening to them and tending to their needs.

The Golden Years

My next posting as Sub-divisional Officer, Banka, in Bhagalpur district, was a mere interlude. In less than a month I was called to the state secretariat to join as an Under Secretary in the Labour Department. Within six months, I moved over as Under Secretary in the combined Irrigation, Electricity, Public Works and Public Health & Engineering Departments—headed by one Secretary and assisted by a Deputy Secretary and two Under Secretaries. To say the least, for all of us it was high-pressure work with not a moment's respite.

I stayed on in the Works Departments for nearly six years at a stretch where, in the meantime, I was promoted as Deputy Secretary. It was only sometime after my promotion to the Indian Administrative Service that I moved out of the Secretariat to join as District Magistrate & Collector of Purnea in July 1957.

My years in the state secretariat were unquestionably the most momentous and formative years of my career as a civil servant. These years reflected the golden age of Bihar administration, but they also witnessed the emergence of forces that set it on the path of uninterrupted decline. Dr. Shri Krishna Sinha, popularly known as Shri Babu, was comfortably in the saddle, holding the reins of the political wing of the government and the party firmly in his hands. With implicit trust reposed in him, Shri Babu left the administrative machinery of government in the care of the Chief Secretary Mr. L.P. Singh I.C.S., who later became Home Secretary in the Government of India and Governor of the North-Eastern States after retirement.

Mr. L.P. Singh has remained a legend in the annals of Bihar's bureaucracy. There was not one aspect of administration that escaped his sharp eyes. His supervision of his officers was such that they would never deliver anything other than their best. The formidable combination of the broad, statesman-like qualities of Shri Babu and the rare comprehension, administrative insight and dedication of Mr. L.P. Singh, his trusted Chief Secretary, earned for Bihar the distinction of being mentioned as one of the best administered states in the country in the report presented by Mr. Paul Appleby, an American expert on public administration.

The departments where I worked were particularly sensitive on account of some special features. The Public Works Department originally embraced all branches of engineering works and its Chief Engineer was also the Secretary to the government. After Independence, the Chief Engineer was replaced by a generalist administrator as the departmental Secretary, causing much heartburn and resentment among the engineering community. On top of it, the recently introduced amalgamated system of secretariat business required technical proposals from the departmental heads to be examined at the government level in the same file in which they originated. The Public Works Department, where the Chief Engineer was designated Secretary ex-officio, was no exception to this new rule. With a generalist Secretary at the helm, any critical comment while examining the Chief Engineer's technical proposals in the same amalgamated file was like adding salt to an open wound. It was natural, therefore, for the engineering community to denounce the new system.

The controversy over whether a specialist or generalist should be the principal policy adviser to government in technical departments has since ceased to excite passionate debate. A more pragmatic approach now appears to guide the decisions of government in specific situations and obviously this makes much better sense. We have seen exceptionally gifted generalist administrators comprehending knotty technical issues in the light of broader policy perspectives and providing balanced advice to the technical wing. Specialists have done no less to elicit the best results from such competent generalist administrators. But both of them, while serving the new political masters, soon discovered that if they must retain their positions they must be able to prove their 'utiliy', which had little to do with their technical expertise or administrative capabilities.

My Secretary was highly assertive when it came to the Public Works Department, but he was a completely different personality as Secretary in the Irrigation and Electricity Departments. Ram Charitra Singh, the Minister in charge, was a most interesting character with sharp idiosyncrasies and a lot of confused thinking. Tall and well-built, with a pair of thickly curled moustaches adorning his chiseled face, he had a rough exterior that concealed a soft heart. He was very close to being quixotic in professing and practicing what he believed, often wrongly, to be the right course of conduct. Having been a lecturer in chemistry in some remote past, he fancied himself as a man of science and, therefore, identified himself with the department's technical and professional staff over whom he reigned as an unchallenged patriarch. Little wonder that he was the butt of many hilarious jokes that gained currency at the time. The Chief Engineer of the Irrigation Department, who was from the Indian Engineering Service, had secured an accelerated promotion with the exodus of British members of the Service and took good care to feed the vanities and foibles of the Minister to become something of a favourite of his. So, there was complete harmony in the working of the Irrigation Department, as both the Secretary and the Chief Engineer saw eye to eye on every issue through the Minister's eyes.

Things went along like this until Mr. Tribeni Prasad Singh became the Secretary sometime in the latter half of 1952. Tribeni Prasad was essentially an intellectual who had found his way into the Indian Civil Service. He did not, however, allow his craving for knowledge to be stifled in the rarefied atmosphere of that 'heaven-born' service. A brilliant student of physics, his quest for pure knowledge spurred him on to study subjects like history and ancient Sanskrit literature. But, despite all these other pursuits, he was down to earth in discharging his professional responsibilities.

In no time, T.P. found himself questioning the technical soundness of some of the proposals sent up by the Chief Engineer for approval of the government. Ram Charitra Singh, the Minister, considered such conduct on the part of a generalist Secretary as unpardonable affront and recorded something in that vein on the files. T.P. Singh remained undeterred and lashed out at whatever he found to be intellectually dishonest.

There was, for instance, a proposal from an Executive Engineer seeking permission to name the design of a weir after the Chief Engineer, which the latter endorsed for government's approval. Mr. T.P. Singh was quick to react. He commented that the abject flattery on the part of the junior officer should have been rebuffed by the Chief Engineer at once as he had had no role to play in the design or construction of the weir. It must be said to the credit of Ram Charitra Singh, who hated sycophancy, that, despite his apparent antipathy for T.P. and partiality for the Chief Engineer, he endorsed the Secretary's comment.

Lacking adequate knowledge and appreciation of the subject, as well as the confidence and will needed to tackle the stupendous problems of providing irrigation facilities for a chronically drought-stricken state, we were struggling to implement only small and inexpensive schemes of dubious merit aimed at providing quick benefits at best. The century-old Sone Barrage, then the only major irrigation system in the state, had already outlived its utility. Some work had been taken up for investigation and appraisal of the Kosi Flood Control and Gandak Irrigation Projects. But, left in the hands of a retired member of the Indian Engineering Service, these initiatives were allowed to languish, which perfectly suited his personal interests. Everybody seemed to be happy: after all, little things go around quicker and farther than the big ones and appease many more political bosses.

Even with the Damodar Valley Project, which was then under execution, our engineers were satisfied — thanks to ineffectual leadership — with putting up diversion weirs here and there which did not demand any great knowledge of engineering or capacity for handling large construction works. We were fed with the myth that in the event of the failure of "hathia" rains (which usually spanned a twelve-day period from the end of September and was nectar for the kharif crop) these weirs would divert the waters, collected during the monsoon rains, and deliver them to the fields. But, with hardly any storage capacity, it was a sheer act of faith to trust in the efficacy of those rudimentary devices.

The annual floods that often visited the Bihar plains close on the heels of cyclical droughts have plagued Bihar for ages. But no major scheme was offered to divert the flood waters into irrigation channels. All we got were higher and higher embankments and, as soon as they gave way, more and more 'retired lines'.

The lack of will on the part of the political masters, obsessed as they were in securing petty gains for their constituencies, combined with the lack of enterprise of top level engineers and the anxiety of the generalist Secretary to play safe, led to the sorry state of affairs. Those were crucial and formative years when the country had launched a programme of planned development through the Five Year Plans, but in Bihar we remained bogged down with short term measures. The sanction of the Kosi Project, thanks to the untiring efforts of Chief Minister Dr. S.K.

Sinha, brought about a renaissance. Due to our level of unpreparedness we had to borrow top level engineers from other states to get the project going.

Mr. T.P. Singh's was the first voice of protest against the prevailing malaise in the Irrigation Department. The Minister Mr. Ram Charitra Singh was soon fuming with rage at the audacity of the generalist Secretary questioning the professional competence and efficiency of his expert engineers and wanted to get rid of him. Mr. T.P. Singh's reaction was typical of the man. He told me that he had abandoned his plan to take long leave for a much needed rest to allow the Minister do the worst that he was capable of. Meanwhile, relations between them deteriorated fast, leaving its imprint on the files. Once, out of sheer spite, the Minister, on one of the files wrote that the Secretary's notes were confusing. Mr. Singh re-submitted the file requesting the Minister to say how and where they were so. Otherwise, he wrote, he would remain 'even more confused'. This time the Minister was truly confused and quietly returned the file without a word other than his signature.

On one such occasion the Minister called me to his official residence and told me to send all files directly to him, without routing them through the Secretary. I told him without a moment's hesitation that I could not do so and that in any case he must pass written orders. The Minister balked, though he appeared impressed by my plain speaking. I told the Secretary what the Minister had asked of me. When he cynically responded with a 'theek hai', I retorted with some anger that even if it was so with him, it was not 'theek hai' with me.

The story has a dramatic end bordering on pathos. The Chief Engineer held a tenured post, with terms of appointment that were renewable at fixed intervals. Predictably, the Minister wanted the incumbent, who had several more years to retire, to continue on the job. A proposal was accordingly sent to the Cabinet, which was promptly turned down. Ram Charitra Singh reacted by resigning from the cabinet and also the party, to contest and win election as an independent candidate. Meanwhile, his favourite Chief Engineer moved to a post of equivalent rank in the Government of India and later found a comfortable berth as Member of the Union Public Service Commission.

I cannot help remembering Ram Chatritra Singh with feelings of respect and admiration for his last quixotic act. There was no restraining him from throwing away an established political career to fight for what he believed was the right thing to do.

At my desk

The Descent Begins

Mahesh Prasad Sinha, a Congressman from a prosperous landholder family of Muzaffarpur, belonged to the Bhumihar caste, the same as Sri Babu's. It was widely known that Sri Babu had a strong personal attachment to Mahesh Babu and his family. That was reason enough for the latter to be much sought after by opportunistic politicians and the general tribe of favour seekers. Soon, Mahesh Babu emerged on the political scene as a force to reckon with.

After the general elections of 1952, the print media published, reportedly on good authority, a list of individuals who were expected to be inducted into the new ministry. Predictably, the list included the name of K.B. Sahay, but there was no mention of Mahesh Babu. K.B. Sahay had enjoyed a prominent position in the last cabinet, was identified as Shri Babu's trusted lieutenant and exercised direct authority over the departments held by the Chief Minister. Some men in the party did not like his meteoric rise and became fiercely proactive. Their efforts succeeded with Mahesh Prasad Sinha's inclusion in the new Council of Ministers. The game of political intrigues was now openly afoot and ruthless internecine feuds never stopped after this, resulting in the rout of the Congress party in the general elections of 1967.

Despite strong divergences of personality and character and their own political rivalry, Mahesh Babu and K.B. Sahay shared a common dislike for the Chief Secretary, Mr. L.P. Singh. Neither of them could freely have their way so long as Shri Babu consulted and deferred to L.P. Singh's advice in all matters concerning the administration in the larger interests of the state. So, when a call came from the Government of India, sometime in 1956, for appointing Mr. Singh as Joint Secretary in the Home Ministry —and Shri Babu expressed unwillingness to part with him, it is believed that it was Mahesh Babu who prevailed upon the Chief Minister to relieve Mr. Singh for his new assignment. Coming at a rather critical juncture, Mr. Singh's departure from Bihar proved to be costly.

K.B. Sahay's exultation in getting rid of Mr. L.P. Singh found expression in a manner that sums up the man. Shri Babu had invited Mr. and Mrs. Singh to a farewell dinner at his residence at which Mr. Sahay was also present. Due to their long association with Shri Babu and their personal regard for him, while taking leave of their host Mrs. Singh mentioned that Shri Babu was welcome to consider staying with them during one of his visits to Delhi. K.B. Sahay promptly interjected, with his characteristic smile that ill-concealed a sneer, to remind Mrs. Singh that they would be living in a small flat in Delhi, not in a mansion as they occupied here in Patna. Where would she find, he asked, the space to have the Chief Minister for a house guest? Shri Babu was aflush with anger and embarrassment and his reply was also typical of his emotional nature. He told Mrs. Singh that even if they stayed in a one-room flat in Delhi, he would be happy to accept their hospitality, pulling out a 'charpoi' for himself.

The general elections of 1957 saw both Mahesh Babu and K.B. Sahay demolished in their respective constituencies, each having spared no effort to see the other defeated. As if this was not enough of a warning, factionalism asserted itself by setting up Anugraha Babu to contest for leadership of the legislature party. The Rajputs were bent upon wresting the party leadership from the ruling Bhumihars. For the first time there was a contest for the office of Chief Minister. The event proved catastrophic, letting loose a chain of reactions which led to the rapid degeneration of politics in Bihar. Inevitably, the malaise crept into the ranks of the administration with disastrous consequences.

Shri Babu won by a comfortable majority, but not without feeling shaken about the assailability of his position. Anugraha Babu died within months of this contest, but K.B. Sahay was now working against the leadership and Shri Babu was well aware of his destructive potential. The political personality of Shri Babu underwent a transformation after this leadership contest. Henceforth, he dedicated himself to the task of consolidating his position so that he would continue to remain the supreme and unchallenged leader of Bihar and also ensuring that the power structure of his regime survived even after he was gone. The choice of a successor had already been made and who else could it be but Mahesh Babu. Willy nilly, for the first time Shri Babu emerged primarily as the leader of the Bhumihars of Bihar. Even so, he carried with him some strong allies from other 'forward' castes, while also rallying the numerically strong 'backward' castes behind him.

It was almost like a Greek tragedy for Shri Babu to fall from his towering pedestal as the supreme leader transcending caste and group affiliations— to the sordid depths of factional politics. But, in the very nature of tragedies, its inevitability was accepted. Factionalism, based on caste loyalties and ruthless political opportunism, was unleashed with a vengeance and soon acquired legitimacy in all aspects of life in Bihar.

Scenes from the District: Factions in Action

As the key functionary and head of the district administration, the slightest tug of factional politics was immediately felt by the head of the district administration. By 1957, I had joined as District Magistrate and Collector of Purnea and was soon moved to Saharsa district in the same capacity. My sudden transfer from Purnea was in itself an outcome of the interplay of factional politics. With Mahesh Babu emerging as Shri Babu's political successor, the battle-lines were getting clearly drawn. The forces opposed to this emerging phenomenon was grouped together under K.B. Sahay, who, for all his organizing skills, was often referred to as Mr. Sampat, named after a slick political operator in a popular comedy of the time. With rare exceptions, Congressmen in the districts aligned themselves with rival political camps, proclaiming their respective loyalties.

At this time, Mr. Shashi Kant Sinha was the District Magistrate of Saharsa. He happened to be a close relative of K.B. Sahay, which was reason enough to brand him as partisan. Mahesh Babu's protégé, Mr. Bhushan Prasad Gupta, a local faction leader belonging to one of the backward castes, who was also Chairman of the District Board, was pitched against

Pandit Rajendra Mishra, a veteran state level Congressman. Bhushan Babu carried his bitter complaints to his patron and succeeded in dislodging the District Magistrate Mr. Sinha.

It was against this background that I was abruptly pulled out of Purnea and sent to Saharsa. Within a day of my reaching there, Bhushan Babu called on me at my temporary abode in the Circuit House to welcome me to the district. My predecessor took a couple of days to wind up and hand over charge. When I went to see him off at the railway station, Bhushan Babu appeared with a thick garland of flowers which he tenderly put around Shashi Sinha's neck.

Pandit Rajendra Mishra came to see me within a few days of my taking charge, making it a point to mention that he had been out of station. He talked about the major problems afflicting the district and also gave some veiled hints about the prevailing political situation. He left me in no doubt about his political stature and his unquestionable superiority in every respect over Mr. Bhushan Prasad Gupta, his one-time lieutenant and now his political adversary.

Both Pandit Rajendra Mishra and Bhushan Babu were frequent visitors to my residential office, but with a difference. Bhushan Babu had been going around giving the impression that I had been sent to Saharsa at his behest to set things right for him. His visits, therefore, were invariably about lobbying for favours to be bestowed on someone or the other. Rajendra Babu came with his list of complaints about things not being done by this or that officer, but he also analysed the problems of the district which was devastated by the ravages of the Kosi - Bihar's 'River of Sorrow'.

My stint in Saharsa began early in the winter of 1958, following a year of the severest of droughts. Babu Rajendra Prasad, President of India, came visiting the drought-affected districts of Bihar, which also brought him to Saharsa. Here he addressed a large public meeting convened by the Bharat Sewak Samaj, an organization of recent origin about which more will be said in the next chapter. Soon after the President began addressing the meeting, a group of men from the audience began shouting slogans against the Bharat Sewak Samaj. The Inspector-General of Police looked at me appearing rather disturbed and apparently expected me to 'do something'. I advised him that we should watch the situation and do nothing more at that stage. In no time, their protest having been registered, the hecklers settled down quietly to listen to the President. Shri Babu was, perhaps for the first time, accompanying the President throughout on this tour. In the midst of his preoccupations, he found time to tell me that things were not going too well in Saharsa and that he would visit it again soon. I sensed the hint of a message.

Sure enough, he flew into Saharsa within a fortnight. True to form, he was late by a couple of hours and I had to detain a train to take him to Madhepura, a sub-divisional headquarter town. From there he went to Singheshwarsthan, where he made offerings at the Shiva temple and moved around the annual fair held there during the period. The return journey from Madhepura was made in a motor trolley provided by the Railways, avoiding the bumpy jeep ride over 25 km of rough and dusty roads. Returning to Saharsa, Shri Babu met party workers over lunch in the local Congress party office. With the day's job over, he got up to leave.

As he was about to depart, Congressmen of both the factions and their leaders closed in on the aircraft to see him off. Before entering the airplane, Shri Babu addressed these last words to me, words that still ring in my ears: "Saharsa is safe in your hands." There was a chorus of assent from Bhushan Babu and his men and an equally eloquent silence on the other side. The words now acquired a quaint suggestiveness and I was left in no doubt why Shri Babu's visit to Saharsa was so urgent.

But, I soon proved to be a disappointment for Bhushan Babu and his men. In preparation for the introduction of the Panchayati Raj System of self-government, the elected District Boards all over the State were taken over by the government around August 1958. Shorn of his office and all his powers to dispense favours, Bhushan Babu was soon being deserted by the self-seeking hangers on. With his hold over party politics of the district thus slipping away day by day, Bhushan Babu sought to save face among his patrons by accusing the district administration of being uncooperative. Pandit Rajendra Mishra was also not happy with me for my policy of severe equidistance. It was not enough that the district was being well administered. To be acknowledged and accepted, one could not afford to be independent and non-partisan.

After having spent more than a year in Saharsa and having handled relief operations on a major scale, which earned some appreciative comments from the state government, I was interviewed by Mr. Shambhunath Jha, then Assistant Editor of the English daily, The Indian Nation. Mr. Jha belonged to Saharsa and liked to stay in close contact with the local politicians. This propensity also earned him a berth in the short-lived Shoshit Dal government, of which we shall hear more later. At the end of our session Mr. Jha told me that he had gone around the district meeting a cross section of people and could testify that I had lived up to my non-partisan credentials as both the warring political factions in the district were abusing me with equal vehemence. This was indeed a highly complimentary assessment in the prevailing circumstances.

Towards the end of my tenure in Saharsa the Chief Minister made one last visit. This time he was remote and cold and I realised that I had failed to deliver what was expected of me.

With Pandit Nehru in Saharsa

The most memorable event of my Saharsa sojourn was the visit of the Prime Minister, Jawahar Lal Nehru, who had come to attend the inauguration of the Kosi Barrage by the King of Nepal. Pandit Nehru alighted from his plane radiating charm and immediately got ready to receive the King whose aircraft was already hovering overhead. Formalities over, the King was escorted to a 'shamiana' pitched on the edge of the landing ground. As cold drinks were being served to the guests, Pandit Nehru was impatiently looking at his watch. Making a note of this, the King stood up and Nehru also sprang to his feet like an uncoiled spring, as if to shake off the lassitude of the past few minutes.

Later in the afternoon, when Pandit Nehru came to the landing ground to bid the King farewell, a large crowd was pressing against the wire fencing erected to keep them at a safe distance. After the royal aircraft took off, Nehru looked around and happily moved towards the cheering crowd. Looking for some kind of a perch, his eyes fell on the mobile ramp parked on the ground and he briskly climbed on to it. From this platform, he waved out and asked the crowd to join him in a chorus of 'Jai Hind'. His every movement was inspirational and perfectly timed. I could feel the air getting charged with something like an electric current, and the crowd burst forth with lusty cheers.

Pandit Nehru then moved up to the plane which was to take him to Patna for the night's halt. The Governor and Chief Minister were to accompany him. Nehru stood at the foot of the ramp waiting for them and his own entourage to get in. Shri Babu held back till the last and invited Pandit Nehru to get in before him. But, in true 'pahle aap' fashion the latter insisted that Shri Babu must enter the aircraft before him. Giving up, and seeing no aide by his side, Shri Babu heroically pulled himself up clutching at the hand rails of the ramp.

The sight reminded me, with a start, of the warning given to me earlier by an aide of the Chief Minister. On failing to find a place for himself in the V.I.P. motorcade, he had warned me that the Chief Minister would be very annoyed if he did not find his aide close at hand, and that I would be held responsible. Shri Babu needed help in climbing up stairs and, particularly, rising from a squatting position. I learnt later that the same aide had somehow managed to reach the Chief Minister just as he was about to climb the stairs of the dais at the public meeting ground. A mishap was narrowly averted.

Kosi Project Department: Some Rare Experiences

I was back in the Secretariat in July, 1959 as Joint Secretary in the Kosi Project Department and soon got promoted as Additional Secretary. For several reasons, a posting in this new Department was then considered a rare privilege. One important reason was the personality and high stock of Mr. Tribhuvan Prasad Singh - popularly known as T.P. Singh Senior — to distinguish him from the other T.P. Singh, who was my Secretary in the Irrigation & Public Works Departments. Senior TP Singh was the Chief Administrator of the Kosi Project and also Secretary to the government in that department. For sheer drive and capacity to conceive, plan and execute large projects he had few equals. His natural flamboyance was accompanied by deft penmanship. It was a treat to read his presentations on technical aspects of project implementation in concise layman's language, highlighting policy aspects that called for urgent decisions at the level of government. As expected, he also had his strong likes and dislikes. But, once he had taken someone under his wing, he would repose implicit trust in him and reach out to offer whatever help he could to promote his protégé's welfare and interests.

When the Kosi Project was taken up for execution around 1955 or 1956, it was found that the contractors had quoted very high rates for earthwork on the embankments. The far flung work sites, lack of communications and the prevalence of diseases, made it extremely difficult to attract professional contractors who could offer competitive rates. In this situation, an idea was mooted to get the work done by mobilizing people's cooperation. This led to two significant developments: emergence of a new leader in Lalit Narain Mishra and creation of a new organization at his instance - the Bharat Sewak Samaj.

In a nutshell, the scheme sought to organize local residents into units and link them with adjoining segments of the flood protection embankment, under the charge of a unit leader nominated by the Bharat Sewak Samaj. The unit leader would mobilise all able-bodied working men of the area to join in the construction of the embankment. The initial capital for this would be advanced by the project office and funds would be replenished as the work progressed, with measurements taken at short intervals. The profits earned would form the corpus of a fund for financing development works in the local areas. The scheme was unique in its scope and the concept was undoubtedly attractive. There was a snag, however. The numerous executing agents would be amateurs picked up from the adjoining villages and, as nominees of an organisation with strong political links, they may not be sufficiently amenable to departmental control. These factors posed a threat to the strict observance of technical standards.

Mr. Gulzarilal Nanda, the then Union Minster for Irrigation, was attracted to the idea as well as its sponsor Shri Lalit Narain Mishra, whose subsequent entry into the corridors of power can be traced to these early developments. But T.P. Singh, who recognised the stakes and was trying to address the valid concerns of his engineers, refused to succumb. Meanwhile, the Prime Minister had also developed a liking for the proposal. The adamancy of the Chief Administrator prompted the Central government to issue a directive for his immediate replacement. Shri Babu did not allow the Central government's directive to slip out of his hands and just sat over it.

Getting an inkling of what was going on, Nandaji invited Shri Babu to a meeting with the Prime Minister and asked him to bring T.P. Singh along. Earlier on the appointed day, Nandaji had a long talk with Mr. Singh after which, as he himself told me, Nandaji sent off a letter to the Prime Minister in which he advised the Prime Minister that they were dealing with an officer who, if properly handled and motivated, could actually deliver the goods. When Pandit Nehru met them, he talked to Mr. Singh softly and persuasively. He said that he looked at the public cooperation programme as a sort of catalyst that could arouse people's awareness of their role in executing development projects and simultaneously offer a constructive work programme for engaging local party workers and keeping them out of mischief. And who else could he turn to for help in such a noble endeavour but to a handful of dedicated civil servants? Small wonder that Mr. Singh became a convert overnight.

Later, when Mr. Singh thanked the Chief Minister for having stood by him, Shri Babu's reply was not only starkly honest but also contained a taste of things to come. He said he did not deserve thanks as he had acted primarily in his self-interest. How could he allow himself to be directed by the Centre in this highhanded manner and yet hold his head high as the Chief Minister of the state?

The Kosi Project offered unique opportunities to an officer to enrich his experiences and broaden his vision. The work spilled over into foreign territory. The project authorities built communication systems, including a railway to carry construction materials from inside Nepal, as well as residential accommodations for the project staff. An agreement with the Government of Nepal provided for setting up of a committee comprising representatives of the Governments of India and Nepal for settling matters of common interests and concerns. Preparations for these committee meetings introduced us to many protocols to which we would have otherwise remained strangers. There were also other problems, the solutions to which called for a wholly unorthodox approach as we were dealing with agencies and institutions of a foreign country. I will recount one instance here.

The project authorities had assigned work to a Nepalese contractor as part of its many goodwill gestures for Nepal. Due to repeated defaults on his part, the contract was terminated. After some time, the contractor filed a suit for damages in a civil court in Nepal, impleading the Chief Administrator. The court's notice was served on him, its validity not yet clearly established. A ticklish point of law arose concerning the jurisdiction of the Nepalese court to try a case involving an official of another sovereign country. Our Ambassador in Nepal, Mr. Bhagwan Prasad Sahay, was inclined to the view that since the act, which was the subject matter of the suit, was not performed in exercise of the sovereign functions of the state, it would not be safe to take the stand on jurisdiction. I was then assigned to study the situation closely and follow it up with our contacts in Nepal. This took me to Kathmandu to parley with Mr. Hareshwar Dayal, who had by then succeeded Mr. Bhagwan Prasad Sahay. Mr. Dayal was his usual urbane and courteous self and spoke with charming candour. Before meeting him, I had already consulted one of the top civil lawyers of Kathmandu whom I had found perched in an attic of sorts, seated on a mat spread over its earthen floor. I had meanwhile also done a survey of the court room from the outside, where the suit would likely be tried. I noticed a rather large-sized bullock guarding the main door of the court room.

I came back resolved not to 'let the law take its course' and proposed a formula for settling the case out of court. The formidable barriers of the Finance Department were easily crossed, thanks to the insight of Mr. Sachin Dutt, Finance Secretary, who had earlier served as Joint Secretary in the Kosi Project Department. We were thus saved from the unpredictable outcome of the litigation, though we certainly missed viewing Nepal's civil court from the inside.

The Gandak Irrigation Project was sanctioned around 1962 and was taken over by the Kosi Project Department, which was re-christened as the River Valley Projects Department. By now we had our own Chief Engineer to take charge of the project activities. Mr. S.A.F. Abbas, my friend of the bridge table and a very dear friend indeed, joined the department as Additional Secretary and the work was divided between us. Very soon, however, both of us began feeling a little uneasy about our respective positions, as some officers junior to us had already been appointed full Secretaries with independent charge of departments. In terms of rank and pay, the posts of Secretary and Additional Secretary in the state were equivalent, unlike those at the centre, but there was a certain loss of status. I spoke to Mr. T.P. Singh candidly about the matter and he fully agreed.

So, early in 1963, when an offer came for a change of assignment, it was quite welcome. As Mr. Singh had already agreed to relieve me, I shifted to the Industries Department to join as Managing Director of the recently constituted Bihar State Industrial Development Corporation.

The Night Descends

Shri Babu was taken seriously ill towards the end of 1960 and passed away on 31st of January of the following year. Deep Narain Singh, Minister of Irrigation, was sworn in as Chief Minister ad interim until the party elected its new leader. Predictably, Mahesh Prasad Sinha staked his claim, which was contested by Pandit Binodanand Jha, and the latter won with comfortable margin. Pandit Jha was re-elected as party leader after the general elections of 1961, but did not survive to complete his full term as Chief Minister. As the story goes, he unwittingly invited the axe of the Kamaraj Plan to fall upon him. Around August 1963 he met Pandit Nehru and told him that being a Brahmin pandit, the powers and trappings of office did not suit his temperament and his cherished goal was to run an institution for educating Congressmen in the political philosophies of Gandhi and Nehru. Soon after this meeting, he was woken from sleep late one morning - being a patient of insomnia he would often sleep late - only to be told that he was among the big twelve who would be called upon to surrender office in order to strengthen the party organization. Alas, Pandit Nehru had taken him at his word.

I had no experience of working closely with Pandit Jha, though I had on several occasions come in contact with him in person and through office files. Pandit Jha had a sharp mind and a remarkable memory, and his reading was varied and extensive. I had heard him speak extempore on two occasions to literary gatherings of Bengalis. He spoke the language fluently and dwelt upon aspects of the social and cultural history of Bengal with the facility of a student of the subject.

Pandit Jha, however, had an overpowering weakness for the famous 'pedhas'of Deoghar which he consumed in large quantities despite doctor's orders. He wanted to see that anyone approaching him with a prayer should return satisfied, confident in the assurance that the prayer would certainly be granted. Very often he would pass written orders in the supplicant's presence, directing the concerned officers to do exactly as requested. Quite as often, though, he would verbally advise the very same officers to take no notice of his written instructions.

My stay in the Bihar State Industrial Development Corporation was cut short when I fell ill and proceeded on leave. K.B. Sahay had already succeeded Pandit Jha as Chief Minister. On the expiry of my leave, he agreed to post me as Secretary of the Welfare Department, which then dealt with welfare measures specifically sanctioned for the benefit of members of the scheduled castes and scheduled tribes and some scholarship schemes for members of 'other backward classes'. The department had been truncated and a retired I.A.S. officer appointed as Secretary of an official committee for monitoring the progress of various departmental schemes where tribals were the beneficiaries. This officer was also made an ex-officio Secretary of the Welfare Department for dealing with specific programmes related to tribal welfare. By common knowledge, this particular officer was being rewarded for 'services' rendered by him in the past. By this time, K.B. Sahay had also gotten rid of Mr. Sachin Dutt, who had been occupying the key post of Finance Secretary. Mr. Dutt was a first class graduate of the London School of Economics, a brilliant officer with an independent and incisive mind. He was first shifted to a relatively unimportant department and, later, quickly relieved when he obtained a posting in the Government of India as Joint Secretary in the Ministry of Finance. Sahay appointed T.P. Singh (Junior) as the new Chief Secretary.

One incident typical of the declining ethical standards and norms of conduct stands out from an episode in the Welfare Department. Mr. P.K. Chaudhary, Under Secretary told me one day that a Member of the Legislative Assembly – he later became a Cabinet Minister – had presented a false bill for attending a meeting of one of the departmental committees. Upon investigation he had discovered that the M.L.A. had also drawn traveling allowance from the Legislative Assembly Secretariat for the same journey for attending a meeting of the House committee. I fully supported the Under Secretary's decision to reject the fraudulent claim. Subsequently, Mr. Chaudhary confessed to me with a pained look on his face that he had passed the false bill after all. He went on to narrate how he had been summoned by the Minister and given a sound drubbing for his 'misguided zeal' and ordered to pass the bill forthwith without any more fuss. Understandably, he could not stand up to the Minister or even dare to bring up the matter to me again. Like our Minister in those days, many in the administration today would consider Chaudhary's initial reluctance as an over-reaction by some naïve officer who took his responsibilities much too seriously.

K.B. Sahay's regime was now in full sway. He was a cynic who believed that money was the source of political power and everything was up for sale. Money was needed to fund hungry legislators who held no office but knew how to strike a deal for lending their support whenever the occasion arose; it was needed to sustain the army of volunteers during the elections and also to provide for something extra; it was needed not only for one's own followers but also for those who were inimical to one's political adversaries. If a portion of the loot found its way to the politicians' private coffers it was all in the game, as the Aiyar Commission later observed.

Any one who had business to do with the government now came prepared with the knowledge that a price would have to be paid for official favours. Not that such practices were wholly unknown in earlier days, but it was systemized and perfected by K.B. Sahay. It was during his regime that we began hearing for the first time about the practice of 'farming out' key posts in the engineering departments, a system that was vastly improved upon by a succession of satraps.

K.B. Sahay was reputed to be an able administrator. But, his enormous craving for power suppressed whatever ethical values he may have possessed, if any. Once he set his heart upon a particular goal, he would not stop to ponder over the means to be employed. Although he was truly the architect of land reforms in Bihar, he did not hesitate to strike a deal with the Raja of Ramgarh by allowing him to retain in his custody the mines that had already vested in the state according to law, only to satisfy his narrow political ends.

The ruthlessness of K.B. Sahay's style of functioning can be illustrated by an incident in which I played a part by sheer coincidence. *The Indian Nation*, a premier English language newspaper, had published a news report alleging that the Chief Minister had personally intervened in favour of a person involved in the illegal offtake of a controlled commodity. Sahay apparently had a satisfactory alibi and decided to seize the opportunity to teach this recalcitrant journal a lesson. So, he directed that the state should institute a criminal case against the publishers of the journal for defamation. But, that was not all. He ordered the Chief Secretary to get the journal's premises searched, ostensibly to seize the 'incriminatory' materials. And he specifically desired that it should be a demonstrable action in which a large contingent of police force should be deployed to surround the premises. Latter day parallels come readily to mind, but, by the norms of our times, this was gross abuse of power meant to overawe the print media. Chief Secretary Mr. T.P. Singh was losing his sleep worrying over the possible repercussions of such high-handed action. At this stage, he called me in.

Mr. Singh gave me the file to study. He knew that Dr. Sachin Sen, then Editor of The Indian Nation, was a personal friend of mine. He told me that as soon as this thought flashed across his mind the night before, he knew he had found the solution to the problem and had lapsed into sound sleep. Could I, he asked, explain the position to Dr. Sen and persuade him to save us all from a potentially dangerous situation? The next morning The Indian Nation published some kind of apology to the effect that the report in question had not been thoroughly verified. Mr. Sahay was left with no option but to call off the police action upon which he had earlier set his heart.

This was the kind of person who was now ruling Bihar, aided by a select band of trusted officers who faithfully executed his every stated and unstated directive. A grey pall descended over the whole administration and frustration gripped those who preferred to remain 'uncommitted'. Slowly, but surely, Bihar was entering into a long dark night.

United Front Government: The Ramgarh Affair

As I was biding my time as Secretary of half a relatively insignificant department, Bihar experienced in 1966 one of the worst droughts in a hundred years, threatening a virtual famine in the year ahead. A Relief Coordination Committtee headed by the Chief Secretary started functioning immediately to draw up, direct and coordinate contingency plans for meeting the impending calamity. By this time, Mr. T.P. Singh Junior had gone away to Delhi and had been succeeded by Mr. K. Raman as Chief Secretary. Soon after joining, Mr. Raman picked me up for appointment as Member-Secretary of the Relief Coordination Committee and notified my transfer to this non-existent post. Meeting him, I got a vague idea of what my duties and responsibilities may entail. As the Relief Coordination Committee did not promise full time work, I offered to perform them in addition to my work as Secretary of the Welfare Department. For some reason, the idea did not appeal to Mr. Raman but, eventually, that became the standing arrangement as he failed to obtain approval for creating a new post.

Reacting to the seriousness of the situation, the Government of India sent an official team headed by the Cabinet Secretary to make an appraisal of our state of preparedness. In the upshot, Mr. Raman, suffering as he was from high blood pressure, proceeded on leave. Mr. B.D. Pande, I.C.S., who had left Bihar some five years ago, was sent back to tackle the emergency, and he took over as Chief Secretary with the upgraded rank and impressive designation of Commissioner General - cum - Chief Secretary.

Then came the general elections of 1967 in which the Congress party was routed in Bihar. K.B. Sahay was defeated in both the constituencies from which he had sought election. In the Patna urban constituency, he was defeated by Mahamaya Prasad Sinha, and the Raja of Ramgarh took care to see that Sri. Sahay's pocket borough in Hazaribagh district did not return him either. In his election speeches to the urban voters of Patna, K.B. Sahay, while releasing all kinds of 'gifts' and promising many more, used to say that a vote for him was a vote for the next Chief Minister. What could Mahamaya give them if he was returned? As if to mock his boast, it was Mahamaya Babu who headed Bihar's first non-Congress government that was installed after the rout of the Congress party. Mahamaya Babu, who was earlier a stalwart of the very same Congress party and president of its state committee, later rebelled against it and became president of the state unit of the Bharatiya Kranti Dal. Although the Raja of Ramgarh was the mainstay of the Bharatiya Kranti Dal and played a key role in the formation of the first United Front government, he allowed his nominee Mahamaya Prasad Sinha to head the non-Congress coalition.

The new non-Congress government, comprising a multiplicity of smaller parties, fortunately had a ready-made common programme for the ongoing relief operations. Starting with some unpractical and populist ideas, it soon settled in and grappled with the evolving situation with utmost energy and efficiency. In the beginning we would be called into the meetings of the Cabinet whenever the relief programmes were taken up for review. The first thing the socialist ministers did was to discard the high-backed, heavily-cushioned chairs of the cabinet room and get them replaced by ordinary wooden chairs with cane seats. When the agenda on relief would be taken up, instead of deliberating with their colleagues, they would turn to face the officers in attendance and start addressing them with much passion in their voices. Soon thereafter, a high-level joint committee representing the centre and the state, headed by Bihar's own Babu Jagjiwan Ram, was constituted to make policy decisions on matters relating to relief and review their implementation. In its very first meeting, Mr. Indradeep Sinha of the Communist party, Minister for Revenue, and Kapildeo Singh of the Socialist Party, Minister for Supply and Commerce, argued the case for a substantial increase in the monthly quota of food grains for Bihar. They made an immediate impact by their comprehensive assessment of the situation and their persuasive debating skills. It needed all the experience of a seasoned negotiator like Jagjiwan Babu to pare down the demands to a level that he would be capable of meeting.

When the relief operations concluded, I was appointed Secretary of a new combination of Departments, namely Forest and Excise, both of which were presided over by Dr. Basant Narain Singh, younger brother of the Raja of

Ramgarh. Dr. Singh had played a significant role in the standing confrontation between the Ramgarh Raj and the Congress party in Bihar. K.B. Sahay, hailing from Hazaribagh district over which the domain of the Ramgarh Raj held sway, had been frequently worsted by the wily strategies of the Raja. Sahay and his cohorts had lost election after election after election, starting with those at the level of the District Board. Known for his zeal for land reforms and for his administrative capabilities and drive, Sri Sahay at some stage had caught Shri Babu's attention and was catapulted to the corridors of power. As minister in successive Congress governments, Sahay had presided over the most important and sensitive portfolio of those days, namely Land Revenue. It encompassed the Mines, Forest and Excise departments. With his dynamic zeal, Sri Sahay had launched a massive land reforms programme, earning for himself the animus of the state's landed aristocracy. He had made it sufficiently clear that he was targeting the Raja of Ramgarh in particular. The forest 'mahals' of the Ramgarh estate, along with many others, had been quickly taken over for management under a special enactment soon after the formation of the first post-independence Congress government. They were so held and thereby saved from wholesale destruction, until they vested in the state under the Bihar Land Reforms Act of 1950. Together with the forests the mines were also appropriated, depriving the Raja of his single largest source of revenue.

The Raja was not one to allow this invasion of his private domain without a fight. He created a number of fake leases to save his mines from being vested in the state and tried his very best to hold on to them. The state challenged the fake mining leases and sought enforcement of the law in a number of title suits. As the suits dragged through the courts, the Raja, strange as it may sound, concluded a deal with K.B. Sahay ending in a so-called compromise. But, failing to get the compromise deal implemented, the Raja obtained a verdict from the court of Additional District Judge, Alipore, Calcutta, which upheld the terms of the compromise and permanently restrained the state from pursuing the title suits against the Raja and his surrogates.

Digressing for a while, I must delve a little more into the murky details of the Ramgarh cases. The events spanned nearly two decades, drawing several political stalwarts in its sweep. The dispassionate and prosaic orders of the Calcutta High Court make for a gripping story as they reveal how the politicians of Bihar, pursuing their personal interests and ambitions with deliberately calibrated steps, chose to turn a blind eye to the concerns and interests of the state.

The fake leases created by the Raja to defeat the provisions of the Bihar Land Reforms Act and save his mines from being vested were challenged by the state in several title suits seeking a definitive judicial pronouncement that these conveyance deeds were "sham, colourable and farzi". By a stroke of luck, the special legal cell set up by the government had come upon vital clues that were assiduously followed up to buttress the state's case. The suits posed a real threat to the Raja and, for a while, he used the processes of law to get them stalled. But, these provided only temporary respite.

Trying to rid the menace for good, the Raja looked at the political scenario of Bihar of the mid-fifties. The Rajputs of Bihar had begun rallying around Anugraha Narain Sinha to wrest power from the Bhumihars who were deeply entrenched in the political and social fields. For the Rajputs it was a case of 'now or never'. The Raja, himself a Rajput, had a substantial following within, as well as outside, his own dominions. An idea was floated that the Raja with his followers would join the Congress party, to tilt the political scales. Anugraha Babu as Finance Minister began sharing the Revenue Minister's view that litigation with the Raja was wasteful. Seeing no future for himself under Shri Babu's leadership after the emergence of Mahesh Babu, K.B. Sahay had already begun cobbling up a new alignment of forces. In this conjunction of forces, K.B. Sahay, the architect Bihar's land reforms, proposed a compromise that would allow the Raja to retain the vested mines and extinguish the title suits filed against him by the state. Though the officials of the Revenue and Finance Departments kept applying the brakes, these efforts ended in a compromise whose terms were recorded by Sri K.B. Sahay in his minute dated 5th May 1957. The Raja signified his acceptance of the terms by his letter dated the 16th July 1957.

The Raja, however, could not cash in on this denouement as opposing political forces nullified the deal which was patently mala fide and legally questionable. Sri. Sahay then took recourse to the Alipore Court for enforcement of the terms of the 'compromise' and, to everybody's amazement, got a decree issued in his favour. The Alipore Judge accepted the proposition that as the Revenue Minister K.B. Sahay had acted with full authority and competence to commit the state to such a compromise. By a stroke of his pen the judge passed orders permanently restraining the state from prosecuting its title suits. Appeal against this decree was filed before the Calcutta High Court.

When Mahamaya Babu, the erstwhile stormy petrel of the Congress party, was catapulted to the office of Chief Minister of the first United Front Government, the Raja decided to deliver his 'coup de grace' and eliminate forever all impediments that stood in his path. He coaxed, cajoled and compelled Mahamaya Babu to order withdrawal of the appeal in the Calcutta High Court.

Mahamaya Babu could not have retained his 'gaddi' for long, as cracks had already started appearing in the United Front Government. This last desperate act precipitated its collapse. Mahamaya Babu who was heading a caretaker government was pursued relentlessly by the Raja, compelling him to rush the Legal Remembrancer to Calcutta in order to have the application brought up for the orders of the High Court. By its orders of 25th January 1968 the High Court granted the prayer for withdrawal of the appeal filed by the state. Almost simultaneously, Mahamaya Babu lost his caretaker status.

Alas for the Raja, his victory once again proved elusive. The Shoshit Dal Government, which succeeded the United Front Government, immediately filed an application before the Calcutta High Court urging that the application for withdrawal of the appeal allowed by the court was the outcome of "mala fide action of some of those in power and authority" and was a "fraud on the court". Granting this application for review of its earlier order, the High Court held that the former Chief Minister had not acted "in the best interests of the state". The state government's appeal against the verdict of the Alipore Court was then heard on merits and allowed in full. The government's suits, throttled for years, were disposed of and decrees passed in favour of the state by the Hazaribagh Subordinate Judge's orders of 25th September 1973, thereby ending a long nightmare lasting over two decades. Meanwhile, the state had already suffered loss of revenues of more than rupees twenty crores and had to approach the court again for its recovery.

The conduct of the Ramgarh cases was directly monitored by Mr. Lal Narain Sinha, who rose to be the Attorney-General of India. He applied his rare legal acumen with meticulous attention to detail in order to checkmate every clever move of the Raja in the courts. In the process, he had to resist the self-defeating actions of the state government, for which he had to battle insinuations against his own conduct.

The civil servants of Bihar rose to the occasion, showing tremendous courage throughout in resisting their political masters and behaved as true custodians of the state's interests. In the midst of the political horse-trading of those dismal days, the Raja staged a comeback in a subsequent coalition government headed by Shri Bhola Paswan Shastri. As price of his support, the Raja coaxed Shri Shastri to yield the Mines portfolio to him, a pitiless act of surrendering the state's interests on the altar of political expediency. Now, as the Minister in charge of the relevant government department, and apparently as a last desperate bid, he called for all the files dealing with the Ramgarh cases. Realising the grave implications of handing over the state's records to the very person against whom the suits were directed, the civil servants took recourse to a subterfuge. They hurriedly removed the files from the offices and then pleaded helplessness, saying that the records were still in the custody of the state's legal counsel in Calcutta. Fortuitously, the government was already breaking apart and, in the next few days, it fell.

Some Experiences of the United Front Government

To resume the narrative of my experiences in the first United Front Government, as Minister in the Forest Department Dr. Basant Narain Singh started with some fixed notions born out of his distaste for the policies and programmes of the earlier Congress governments. After all, how could he forget that the forests that had vested in the state were erstwhile properties of the Raj? He began by putting forth several populist ideas, such as pulling down of all fences except those erected around newly planted areas, planting fruit trees inside notified forests, releasing barren forest lands for cultivation and re-opening old cases whereby private lands had been notified as protected forests. Once, he also expressed annoyance over trench-fences dug around newly planted areas, complaining that cattle trying to graze in those areas often got injured when they fell into the trenches. That said, Dr. Singh was intelligent, urbane, friendly and receptive and we immediately struck a cordial note. With this initial advantage, I succeeded in moderating some of his half baked ideas and made him amenable to sane advice which, of course, had to be packaged neatly and presented as a meticulously reasoned product. Some of the development schemes sponsored by him were basically sound, such as construction of diversion dams on 'nullahs' running inside the forests, and we went all out to implement them, mobilising the required funds from different sources.

In fairness to Dr. Singh, I must concede that his 'pastoral' approach to promoting the economic well being of tribal populations, whose lives were intimately woven around the forests in their midst, was shared by many other political stalwarts of the time. The short-term remedy of releasing forest lands to appease the land-hunger of growing human settlements also readily appealed to politicians of all hues. Presiding over a meeting of the Central Board of Forestry at Bangalore in 1968, Babu Jagjiwan Ram made a similar plea as the Union Minister of Food and Agriculture. When Mr. S.P. Shahi, our Chief Conservator of Forests, rose to point out the errors and risks of such a policy, Jagjiwan Babu met his arguments with a huge show of temper. A year or so later, the Communists of Champaran district threatened a movement demanding that some of the swampy patches of the Madanpur Forests should be released for cultivation—as if crops could be raised where trees had failed to find roots.

The programme of stimulating the growth of tribal economies by setting up of forest-based industries has still not found firm footing as an effective policy initiative. Even after sal seeds became a precious commodity as a source of non-edible oil, long-term leases for their collection used to be given at throwaway prices and clauses in the lease agreements mandating establishment of oil extraction plants were quietly by-passed. Early attempts to set up cottage and small industries based on forest products, such as timber treatment, match-making, rope-making and the like, did not develop into a viable programme for want of sustained policy support.

It was love at first sight with the Forest Department for me. Very soon, I developed almost the same protective feelings for the forests as the Chief Conservator of Forests nursed at the end of his long career. Having been in the saddle for seven long years, the Chief Conservator Mr. Shahi had another eight years or so to go before retirement. On top of it, he had superseded one of his seniors in the service who nursed a silent grouse throughout by just staying on as deadweight. Over the years, Mr. Shahi had also developed some pronounced likes and dislikes. Conditions were rife, therefore, for the emergence of a disgruntled group of officers who, for one reason or the other, felt unhappy with his seemingly interminable reign. Not unaware of the situation, the Minister began his term with a prejudice against the Chief Conservator, of which he made no secret.

Putting our heads together, Mr. Shahi and I had scraped up some funds for building a truly attractive Tourist Lodge with modern fittings and facilities within the National Park in the Betla forest range in Palamau district. Mr. Shahi chose the site for the lodge on a mound overlooking the Park, close to its entrance. At about the same time the Minister paid a visit to the area. For some reason, fortunately as it would appear, Mr. Shahi had not accompanied him on this tour. The Minister fancied a site rather deep inside the Park near a flowing stream as he was genuinely impressed by the surroundings. So, he announced his preference on the spot and some of the forest officers accompanying him, and who were only too anxious to please the Minister, vociferously endorsed his choice. Unfortunately, the Minister's preference had not taken into consideration the practical difficulties of providing various services to a standalone building deep inside the forest. Most of all, erecting a building for accommodating tourists in the heart of the Park would disturb the peace and tranquility of the sanctuary. Getting some inkling of the Minister's mind and fearing that he may not be willing to change it, Mr. Shahi rushed in to get the construction of the lodge started on his chosen site before he could be officially directed otherwise. He also enticed me to visit the site to review the progress of the work. I could see what had happened and felt a little disturbed. When he came to know of it, the Minister was infuriated and regarded Mr. Shahi's action as a personal affront. All my pleadings were of no avail. He was determined to start departmental action against Shahi for disregarding his known preference, which I succeeded in stalling for some time. Just at this juncture, the government fell and President's rule was expected to be announced any day. Getting ready to quit, the Minister told me one day with an ironic chuckle that now that I would be functioning virtually as a Minister under President's rule – such was the general belief at that time – I would no doubt drop the action he had proposed against Mr. Shahi!

A major achievement of the United Front Government was the setting up of a Commission of Inquiry presided over by Mr. T.V.L. Aiyar, a retired Judge of the Supreme Court, to inquire into the long list of allegations against some Ministers of the Congress governments of the past.

This was a historic event, for Congressmen - and not only in Bihar - had become so used to power they could never contemplate that they could be thrown out of office some day and that their actions subjected to investigation by a successor government. The Aiyar Commission specifically indicted K.B. Sahay, Mahesh Prasad Sinha and Raghavendra Narain Singh, a State Minister in the outgoing Government, and all of them eventually had to face criminal prosecution. Several officials who were arraigned for having facilitated the impugned acts came severely to grief, faced protracted departmental enquiries and were retired compulsorily, with or without criminal prosecution. Despite the lessons of the Aiyar Commission of Inquiry, malpractices of the kind detected and indicted in its findings have found deeper roots. Only, the strategies have become more refined and a general cult of amorality now pervades public life.

The Shoshit Dal Government, which succeeded the United Front Government, still holds the record as a government where every member of the party was appointed minister. The support of the forty "committed" members of the fledgling party was brought about by the wily K.B. Sahay. My Minister, who had the distinction of having worked his way up from the level of office superintendent in his earlier avatar, confided in me that, despite popular perception, they had taken the oath of office to actually catch the thieves, belying the story of Alibaba and his forty thieves. The first thing that this Government did, obviously as a command performance, was to set up a Commission of Inquiry against some Ministers of the United Front Government in retaliation against the constitution of the Aiyar Commission.

By now, Mr. Bhola Paswan Shastri had risen in revolt against the Congress party and walked out of it with some of his followers in protest against its policy of stark opportunism in setting up the puppet minority government. The Shoshit Dal Government did not last even for two months. But, before it fell, it served as an instrument of public good. It moved the Calcutta High Court for revocation of its orders allowing withdrawal of the state's appeal in the Ramgarh case.

First President's Rule: A Succession of Governments

A Presidential proclamation under Article 356 of the Constitution put an end to the game of making and breaking governments and, early in the summer of 1968, the first round of President's rule was imposed in Bihar. Mr. M.S. Rao, a retired member of the I.C.S. from the Bihar cadre and its one time Chief Secretary and Mr. Anand, a retired Chairman of the Central Water and Power Commission, were appointed Advisers to the Governor.

An exercise was immediately undertaken to draft new Rules of Executive Business. The Chief Secretary Mr. Sohoni sent a draft directly to the Governor, smuggling in a proviso that where the Advisor differed with the Chief Secretary, the matter would go to the Governor for a final decision. Mr. Rao was furious when he saw the draft Rules. In his comments on the draft he reminded the Governor that they were Advisors to the Governor and not to the Chief Secretary. The offending provision was dropped and Mr. Rao, with Mr. Anand 'assisting' him, took up the serious business of governing Bihar. Mr. Rao once confided in one of my colleagues that although he had taken a heavy load of work upon himself, he also enjoyed functioning like a 'nawab', to be able to decide the fate of millions with a mere stroke of his pen.

In less than six months, I was transferred as Secretary of the Irrigation and Electricity department which was placed under the Advisor Mr. Anand. Much as I regretted parting company with the Forest Department, I took an immediate liking for Mr. Anand's habit of treating the Secretary as an equal. Even otherwise, I was in my element in the Irrigation and Electricity Department where I had spent my growing up years in the secretariat.

President's rule did offer scope for untying a few knots. A dispute over seniority involving two groups of senior engineers of the Irrigation Department had been hanging fire for nearly a decade and had, by this time, reached a critical stage. The officers were exercised over it, much to the detriment of the department's normal functioning, as several Ministers had passed divergent orders on considerations which appeared highly subjective and motivated. It needed the respite of President's rule to put an end to this unending see-saw game. I devoted my attention to resolving the contentious seniority issue and bringing it to a conclusive end. As expected, a writ petition was filed against the government's decision, but it was confirmed by the High Court and upheld in appeal by the Supreme Court, setting the final seal over a long festering dispute.

The process of obtaining clearance for any irrigation scheme often involved long inter-departmental file notings, causing undue delay. What was worse, the priorities sometimes got warped due to the special interests of some people who held positions of influence. S. Prabhakaran, who was working with me as Deputy Secretary and N.K. Singh, Deputy Secretary in the Finance Department - son of T.P. Singh (Senior) - put their heads together and produced a precise formula based on the ratio of the cost to the 'social' benefits of any proposal, which was accepted as a firm guideline for processing and sanction of irrigations schemes in the future. I am informed that the formula has survived to this day.

In the Electricity Department, we were soon overtaken by a set of demands served by workers of the State Electricity Board, which led to a notice of strike scheduled to commence just on the eve of elections to the State Assembly in January 1969. We got ready to face the strike which appeared unavoidable. In this context, the Advisors wanted to apprise the Governor of the emerging situation. The Chief Secretary Mr. Sohoni and I were asked to participate in the discussions with the Governor. At the appointed hour, when we were waiting in the ante chamber of the Governor's office, we saw Mr. Rao walk past. Noticing us there, the first thing he said while addressing Mr. Sohoni was that we should wait until we were sent for. Mr. Sohoni visibly flushed at this cavalier treatment. As Mr. Rao entered the Governor's office, he asked me to follow him in. I found Mr. Rao had just settled down and Mr. Anand was seated quietly beside him. Mr. Rao opened the topic for discussion in his leisurely, drawling style, filling his pipe and striking matches all the while in an attempt to light it. Sensing that the discussion was tending to become a discursive slow-motion performance, I plucked up the courage to seek the Governor's permission to butt in even as Mr. Rao was holding forth. Being naturally better prepared with the facts, I was able to pin-point the issues for decision and the meeting ended in no time, with foregone conclusions.

A new political government was sworn in after the Assembly elections. One Chief Minister followed another in quick succession in a period spanning less than six months. The Raja of Ramgarh had staged a comeback, playing an important role in the formation of the coalition government headed by Shri Bhola Paswan Shastri. I have already alluded to the denouement of this short-lived government. After its fall, a second round of President's rule commenced, to end early in 1970 when a third Congress government headed by Daroga Rai was sworn in.

Meanwhile, I had moved to Muzaffarpur as Commissioner of the Tirhut Division. It comprised, at that time, the original districts of Muzaffarpur, Saran, Champaran and Darbhanga, covering almost the whole of Bihar north of the Ganges, except Purnea, Saharsa and parts of Bhagalpur and Monghyr districts. Daroga Prasad Rai came from Saran and belonged to an important backward caste of Bihar, the Yadavs.

During my tenure as a Divisional Commissioner, the Bihar unit of the Communist Party of India started what was called a 'land grab' movement. Their avowed aim was to recover illegally held lands from the big landholders, whether in excess of the prescribed ceiling or by sheer appropriation of public lands. In Champaran district, large chunks of government land had been encroached upon over a long period and eventually integrated with the private holdings of big landlords. The Collector of Champaran, Mr. Shri Vallabh Saran had, with remarkable thoroughness, succeeded in identifying large areas of such encroachments. There were, however, serious hurdles in recovering these lands, and we knew that the process would inevitably get enmeshed in protracted litigation.

Daroga Prasad Rai, having struck some kind of deal with the Communists, desired that we should provide demonstrable support to the land grab movement. It was our intent as well to support the movement's legitimate and substantive goals, but we were equally concerned that the laws should not be openly violated. So, against the backdrop of the threats held out by the land grabbers and armed with land records ferreted out by the district administration, the Collector of Champaran kept up the pressure and succeeded in persuading the big land-holders of Champaran to voluntarily surrender large areas of illegally occupied land. No doubt, the operation was not entirely successful, but a good beginning was made which resulted in substantial gains for the government. Additionally, we succeeded in containing a movement that threatened to break-down law and order on an extensive scale.

As the Divisional Commissioner, I was in the thick of it all. None knew it better than Mr. Chandra Shekhar Singh, then Revenue Minister, with whom I had been in close consultation throughout. Mr. Singh was young, perhaps the youngest member of the Cabinet, and yet he was sober, sound and practical. Above all, he had a genuinely progressive outlook. He also had a good academic record and had kept up his habit of serious reading to improve his mind and add to his storehouse of knowledge. I also had the advantage of enjoying the confidence of the leadership of the state unit of the C.P.I. which averred that I was completely free from any pro-landholder bias.

It was in this setting that the Chief Minister was holding a discussion one day in the Motihari Circuit House, in the heaquarters of Champaran district, poring over some details with the Collector and some revenue officials who had arrived from Patna. The Revenue Minister was also present. The discussion covered grounds which we had traversed over and again, and as there was nothing more for me to add, I sat through the proceeding as a silent observer. Daroga Prasad Rai, attributing my silence to possible indifference, broke in to say that the 'Commissioner Saheb' should take some interest in the matter. The Revenue Minister promptly intervened to say that the Commissioner Saheb was actively behind all that was being done. Daroga Rai mumbled something incoherent and had to eat his words. But, I could see that he did not relish the protestation of the Minister and opted to remain unimpressed, for there was a background to it.

Sometime soon after Daroga Rai had entered office as Chief Minister and during one of his tours to his home district, he had displayed a flash of anger in full public view at the way the local administration was handling the labour strike at the Morton factory. Some of Rai's men had seized the opportunity to get involved in the ongoing industrial action and had been quickly won over by the management, a fact which could not have been unknown to the Chief Minister. As the pro-strikers were being supported by a political party in opposition, the issue had been deliberately confused and politicised. Mr. Rai wanted to maintain a non-partisan posture in public by showing genuine concern with the striking workers, while at the same time hoping that his pro-management followers would not be allowed to fail. To make an impression, and simultaneously creating a diversion, he asked me to look into the matter personally and send my report to the government at once. A plane was flown down from Patna to take me from Muzaffarpur to the district headquarter town of Chapra, from where I moved to the factory premises to make a spot enquiry and assess the situation. In my report, though quite aware of the existing political alignments and overtones, I did not mince words and proposed stringent action against the management. Not impressed by my unimaginative conduct, Daroga Prasad Rai decided that I was not the person who could be worthy of his confidence.

Within barely six months of my stay at Muzaffarpur, some personal problems cropped up which demanded my return to Patna. When I met the Chief Minister to request for a short leave and posting at Patna at the end of it, he immediately agreed to grant me the leave. So, in September 1970, after spending about ten months as Commissioner of Tirhut Division, I went on leave with good reason to believe that I would not be asked to return to my post.

From Pillar to Post

The post of Mines Commissioner in the Department of Mines and Geology was due to fall vacant around the time I would return from leave. The incumbent, Mr. Satish Chandra Mishra, had insisted on availing of leave due to him preparatory to his retirement. Had this leave been refused, as invariably was the established practice, he would have stayed on for four more months and, at the end of it, drawn leave salary instead of pension for the period that leave was refused. Many spirited officers mellowed in their twilight years just so as to 'earn' government's refusal of leave preparatory to retirement, which meant an extra ten thousand rupees or so before the reduced pension benefits kicked in. Thanks to the subsequent expansion of retirement benefits, a retiring officer now gets cash compensation as a matter of right for foregoing the leave due to him preparatory to retirement.

Dr. Nagendra Jha, Minister for Mines and Geology, was on a tour of Muzaffarpur and I met him to enquire if it was true that Mr. Mishra was vacating the post of Mines Commissioner. He responded by saying that if I was interested he would take me in that post. Dr. Jha, a onetime Professor, enjoyed a decent reputation and I had no hesitation in signifying my assent. So, I went on leave from Muzaffarpur feeling assured that I would return to Patna at the end of it. As I was spending the last few days of my leave at Ranchi, a telephone call came from the

Chief Secretary, Mr. R.S. Mandal, and I went to receive the call hoping to hear the expected news.

Mr. Mandal was then officiating as Chief Secretary and was very soon promoted to the substantive post, superseding a number of his seniors. A protest delegation was led to the Chief Minister and it was followed by a writ petition in the Patna High Court, which held that the government was fully competent to appoint any officer to a 'selection post' such as that of Chief Secretary. And yet, some four years later when a Chief Secretary was similarly appointed by superseding some officers senior to him, there were covert protests and widespread discontent. Over the years, and with the experience of the emergency and thereafter, the civil servant now cynically accepts supersession in his stride and is content with protecting his pay and seldom makes it a prestige issue. Acceding to the dictates of the ruling masters has quietly become the established norm and principal criterion for appointment to key positions.

One of Mr. Mandal's many qualities was that of being helpful to his colleagues. Aware of the fact that my aged parents lived in Ranchi, he asked me whether I would like a posting in Ranchi as the Member-Secretary of the Chotanagpur and Santhal Parganas Autonomous Development Authority. This organisation was of recent origin, set up by the Government as a concession to the periodic demands raised for a separate Jharkhand state. By common consent, the organisation was neither autonomous nor did it have any authority. The super-time scale post of Member Secretary in the organisation was just ornamental. I declined the offer but refrained from bringing up the impending vacancy in the Mines department, as it was obvious that something was amiss.

I landed in Patna in a few days to learn that the Cabinet had already appointed me as Mines Commissioner. When I met the Chief Secretary, he asked me to join immediately without waiting for the government's notification, as the Minister was anxious to ensure that the decision was quickly implemented. When I met the Minister after assuming charge, he revealed that the Chief Minister had been pressuring him to accept his nominee and he had to be rather firm to resist him. He felt relieved that I had already assumed charge of the post. I found working with Dr. Nagendra Jha extremely harmonious and pleasant, but he left the government within six months, jolting the apple cart of popular government yet again.

As Mines Commissioner, I soon found that the entire focus of the Department was on granting mining leases which was viewed as dispensation of favours. All my efforts were, therefore, directed at ensuring that the transactions remained above board. Fortunately for me, successive Ministers I had the privilege to work with, namely Dr. Nagendra Jha, Bijoy Kumar Mitra and Bhola Paswan Shastri, who had retained the Mines portfolio for himself in his second term as Chief Minister, were all fair and correct in their dealings and I had no trouble whatsoever in discharging my responsibilities.

The Mines Department and its Chief Executive, the Mines Commissioner, aided by a Director of Mines, and assisted by Deputy Directors and District Mining Officers, had little to do with the actual task of developing the mineral wealth of Bihar, which was second to no other state in the country. We were merely granting mining leases and collecting royalties from the lessees, without even establishing a statutory framework for assessing the demand. Coming within List I of the Seventh Schedule of the Constitution, the regulation of mining rights, leases and royalty for major minerals was remotely controlled by the Union Government. The political stock of Bihar having plummeted, there was little that we could do to make ourselves heard in these matters. I rushed through a proposal to set up a Minerals Development Corporation in the public sector but it took several years to come into being as a functioning organisation. In our time, therefore, we were content to remain only a weak and ineffective revenue-collecting agency. I had given expression to my woes on some occasion to Mr. Mandal. So, when the occasion arose, he asked me if I would like to change over as Commissioner of Commercial Taxes. I agreed and joined that post around November, 1971. Within a few weeks, Bihar was again placed under President's rule.

The Governor under President's rule was Mr. Debkanta Barua. His 'darbari' style of functioning was captured in the pen picture drawn in Janardan Thakur's book: 'All the Prime Minister's Men'. Unlike any of his predecessors, he set up office in a room of the Secretariat, holding court through the office hours, calling up officers, discussing and talking and talking and discussing all the while. Having passed on an idea, he could not refrain from peering at the official notes recorded in the relevant files. Once, while waiting for his plane at the landing ground at Jamshedpur, where some top executives of the principal industrial houses of the city were present to see him off, Mr. Barua announced with evident pride that he never read anything that was not in print. One irrepressible fellow from among them could not help blurting out: "God help Bihar ", earning a hard stare from the Governor.

Mr. Debkanta Barua did not bother to hide his anxiety about the prospects of the Congress party in the coming elections and made pointed enquiries on the subject from the local officers whenever he went out touring the state. Once during one of Indira Gandhi's election tours of Bihar, he hosted a formal reception in honour of the Prime Minister. While he was being advised by his Secretary that he should take care that the event was not interpreted as political kowtowing, Mr. Barua told him: "Mr. Chakravarty, you should know that a tree has to be watered at its roots."

Mr. Debkanta Barua evinced keen interest in raising the state's revenues and rightly considered commercial taxes as the most important source. I had already applied my mind to outlining a scheme for reorganization of the department but had failed to get any encouraging response from the powers that be. I seized this opportunity to tell the Governor that if my reorganisation proposals were approved, I could guarantee a sizeable increase of revenue. He welcomed the idea without, of course, bothering to acquaint himself with any of its details or even its rationale, and wanted the proposal to be submitted for his approval forthwith. I went ahead drawing up an elaborate memorandum, ignoring the Financial Commissioner's advice to go slow. Thanks to all my efforts, the reorganisation scheme with clearly defined yardsticks has remained the basis for the uninterrupted expansion of the department and its revenues.

The general elections of 1972 brought in a Congress government led by Kedar Pandey. Daroga Prasad Rai meekly accepted joining the new team headed by one of his erstwhile colleagues. Rai got the Finance portfolio, which included commercial taxes. So, we were working together again and much closer than before.

When he addressed officials of the two departments immediately after assuming office, Daroga Rai expressed his anxiety to eliminate delays for which the Finance Department was commonly blamed. He followed this up by setting down his 'three-day rule', according to which any matter on which he specifically asked for information or comments must reach him within three days. Once he asked for comments on some proposals for the revision of rates and slabs of agricultural income tax. Nearly a day and half had already been lost before his minute reached us. We rushed along, digging out the old files where the rationale for the current tax rates had been laid out, and then proceeded to analyse the possible outcome of the proposed modifications. As we submitted our detailed analysis a couple of days past the prescribed three-day timeline, the Minister had nothing to say about the merits of the analysis but chose to reprimand us for the delay. I soon discovered that the Minister used the three-day rule as a handy stick with which to beat the officials.

In his inaugural meeting I argued that in a department responsible for collecting sizeable revenues for the state, the chief executive should have the freedom to utilize his officers according to his best judgment. This, I argued, was essential in order to deliver optimum results. The Minister remained silent, but I could clearly gauge that the maxim *'maunam sanmatilakshanam'* - silence denoting consent - did not apply to this matter.

Very soon, in the interest of expeditious disposal, the Minister issued instructions asking for proposals from the Commissioner, except those concerning policy matters, to be submitted to him directly and not routed through the Finance Commissioner. Though this was contrary to the Rules of Executive Business, the Financial Commissioner preferred to let it pass. I had, however, reason to feel uneasy. A large portion of my work concerned cadre management, particularly transfers and postings of officers. As the Finance Commissioner never differed with me in these matters, the Minister had to contend with what were practically our joint recommendations. If I went by the Minister's advice I would have deal with him all by myself without any support in matters where the politician's appetite is insatiable. I, therefore, had no illusions about where all this would lead to.

The Minister once asked me – responsible, as he said, he was to the people - how could he justify the rationale for transfers and postings of departmental staff to the people's representatives. I answered his rhetorical poser by suggesting that he could cite administrative discretion exercised by the chief executive entrusted with direct responsibility for the department. I could sense that the Minister intensely disliked this response, but he could not argue the point. On another occasion, when two circles were carved out of the existing Dhanbad circle and I redistributed the work among the two Assistant Superintendents by shifting one of them to the newly created circle, he asked me to justify the 'transfer'. The work redistribution had removed some 'paying' assessees from the jurisdiction of one of his favourite officers, which was done deliberately and the Minister was quite aware of its implications. When he observed that in this case of transfer I had neglected to obtain government orders, I pointed out that this was not transfer except in a narrow, technical sense. There was no change of station, not even a shift from one room to another in the same office building, but only some administrative redistribution of work. The officers concerned, I maintained, were not affected as in a regular transfer. The Minister suggested that work reorganisation also had severe consequences for the affected officers, something that obviously I failed to appreciate. The innuendo could not be missed. In disgust, I went back and submitted the file to him, offering to make the changes 'as desired' by him. But, he refrained from making any change at this stage. The norms of executive business had not entirely disappeared, especially among the seasoned politicians.

The Minister thereafter sharpened his criticism of the 'delays' and began making some digs. After things had gone along like this for some time, I confronted the Minister one day and asked him if I still enjoyed his confidence. Of course, he protested loudly, but in the next few days he made more barbed comments. I realised that it was time for me to part company from him. I went and talked things over with Mr. P.K.J. Menon, who had returned to Bihar as Chief Secretary under the new government, and asked for permission to proceed on long leave, which was the only form of protest left for me to register. When my leave application reached the Minister, he was full of sympathy for my personal health problems. The stress under which I was working had taken a toll on my health and any further stress was unbearable. So, early in June, I proceeded on leave for four months.

Aware of the circumstances in which I had proceeded on leave, Mr. Menon after a while proposed that I may be recalled for posting as Chief Administrator of the River Valley Projects Department. Having agreed to the proposal in the sub-committee of Ministers dealing with transfers and postings of senior officials, Daroga Prasad Rai sprang a surprise at the cabinet meeting. When the proposal for my appointment in the River Valley Projects was formally placed before the cabinet, he observed that I should not be disturbed by recalling me from leave. Mr. Menon now realised that I had incurred the displeasure of a powerful Minister and would have to pay the price for my obstinacy.

However, before my leave was fully spent and, upon expressing my willingness to return to work, Mr. Menon had me fixed up in the inconspicuous post of Additional Relief Commissioner, which was created for a short duration in the wake of another spell of drought. My Minister was Mr. Chandra Shekhar Singh with whom I had already built up a certain rapport and I passed six uneventful months, having meanwhile moved to occupy the substantive post of Relief and Rehabilitation Commissioner.

At this juncture it was reported in the local Press that the cabinet had ordered my transfer to the post of Member-Secretary of the Chotanagpur and Santhal Parganas

Autonomous Development Authority. Mr. Menon had earlier sounded me about this post and, considering my reservations, had assured me that I would not be disturbed. But, apparently, he had changed his mind and given up trying to salvage me. I sought a meeting with him but was disposed of rather brusquely. I then decided I was left with no option but to speak to the Chief Minister directly.

When I met Mr. Kedar Pandey, he immediately saw that there was a problem in dispatching me for this relatively insignificant assignment. After verifying that the officer earmarked for posting as Divisional Commissioner at Ranchi was junior to me in the service, he agreed that it would be quite inappropriate to send me to occupy a minor post in the same station. After ascertaining my willingness, he picked up the telephone and told Mr. Menon to post me as the Divisional Commissioner instead. I felt vindicated and reassured that my stock had not depleted altogether. I was also touched by the understanding and sympathy coming from a politician. Things moved fast thereafter and, in less than a week, I drove up to Ranchi to assume charge as Commissioner of Chotanagpur Division.

The Land Beautiful and Endless Exploitation

The undivided Chotanagpur Division was the largest of the four original divisions of the State, extending over some 62,000 sq km, comprising nearly two fifths of Bihar's land area. It comprised five of its 17 original districts before the reorganisation. The tribal population of the state is concentrated almost entirely in Chotanagpur and the contiguous Santhal Parganas district of Bhagalpur Division. In Ranchi district the tribals made up nearly 58 per cent of the population, with Singhbhum district sheltering some 46 per cent. This region also contains almost all the mineral wealth of Bihar and many of its industries, particularly the large ones. The Tata Iron and Steel Company at Jamshedpur is the first private sector steel plant in the country; the largest public sector steel factory is situated at Bokaro in Dhanbad district; the first fertilizer plant in the public sector is located at Sindri, near Dhanbad; the largest Heavy Engineering Corporation of Asia is at Hatia on the outskirts of Ranchi. Large mining industries dealing with coal, iron ore, copper, mica, limestone and bauxite are all located in this region.

The Chotanagpur plateau, with rolling green hills and undulating valleys, interlaced with meandering hilly streams and forests covering about two-fifths of its surface, is a land of captivating beauty. The simple lives of tribals in their peaceful homeland had come under tremendous pressure with the surging tide of industrialisation, adding to their age-old exploitation. The administrative tasks of the region were indeed unique and challenging.

Within barely a couple of days of my joining the Division, news reached us about a police firing at Bokaro, causing the death of some workers of a sub-contractor of the Bokaro Steel Project. Arriving there on the following day along with the Deputy Inspector General of Police, Mr. Rajdeo Singh, we held a spot enquiry into the incident. The victims of the firing were tribal men and women who were being cheated of their wages and had been provoked into acting in a fit of rage. This provided the opportunity to the local sub-inspector of police, who had befriended the sub-contractor, to precipitate the crisis. The Magistrate, lacking a sympathetic attitude and acting without foresight and imagination, did the rest by ordering the police to open fire.

As we were getting ready to return to Ranchi on the following morning, a telephone call came from Hazaribagh. The Deputy Commissioner informed me that some incidents of communal nature had occurred there the previous day but there had been no recurrence since. The trouble had occurred, as we learnt later, when a truck accompanying the Ramnavami procession was driven into a piece of land over which there had been a protracted dispute between two communities. Feelings were already wounded by a very recent judicial pronouncement and the recalcitrant truck was the last straw.

On reaching Hazaribagh around noon, we were informed that no further incident had occurred on that day; but looking closely at the situation we could foresee portents of a major flare-up. Our worst fears, unfortunately, came true and several incidents occurred in the dark of the night. As we stayed on to deal with the developing situation, incidents kept erupting here and there, soon reaching some villages around Hazaribagh town. Police forces under magistrates requisitioned from different districts of the Division fanned out to arrest the spread of communal clashes. Despite all our combined efforts, it took us not less than ten days to restore law and order and peace.

News reached us one morning of an incident of arson in a village not far away which had a mixed population of Hindus and Muslims. On reaching there we gathered that the Muslims had already left the village with the outbreak of the trouble and the arsonists had set fire to their abandoned houses. Some neighbourhood dwellings belonging to Hindus had also suffered collateral damage as they could not escape the leaping flames. We were escorted to a shack belonging to a Hindu where a woman had been burnt alive. The owner of the shack could rescue his few belongings but it was too late when it was the turn of his invalid mother.

In the midst of the riots, I got a message that Prime Minister Indira Gandhi would be landing at Ranchi airport for a change of aircraft on her way back to Delhi. I drove to Ranchi early in the morning to be present on the occasion. The local journalists had assembled at the airport and did not miss the opportunity to ask her a few questions. Mr.

N.E. Horo M.P. was then leading the agitation for a separate Jharkhand State. It was reported that Mr. Horo had met the Prime Minister a few days ago and the news had spread. The journalists took the cue and the questions and answers went somewhat like this:

> Journalist: Did Mr. N.E. Horo meet you recently?
> PM: Hundreds of people meet me every day.
> Journalist: What do you think of the demand for a separate Jharkhand state?
> PM: Think? Can you not think for yourselves?

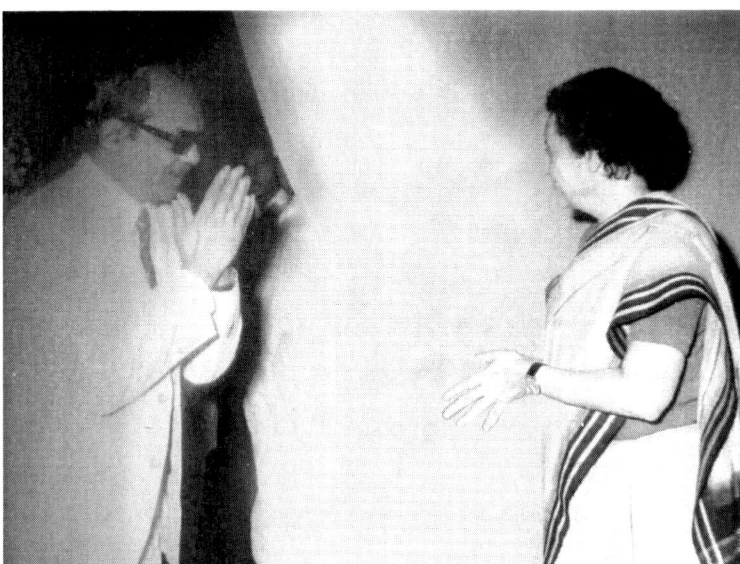

Receiving PM Indira Gandhi at Ranchi airport

The demand for a separate Jharkhand State had been voiced, though somewhat faintly, early in the 1930s. The agitation was muffled with the merger of the Jharkhand party with the Congress party, which had successfully wooed the Jharkhand leader Jaipal Singh into its fold. The truce, as it were, was destined to be short-lived. The demand kept cropping up every now and again. At this juncture, Mr. N.E. Horo was leading some kind of agitation and, from time to time, Mr. Bagun Sombrai from Singhbhum gave him support. Despite all these and the patch-work of development measures undertaken by the state government, the exploitation of tribals continued unabated. The village money-lender deprived many of them of their small parcels of land, the forest contractors cheated them of their wages and the age-old feudal system kept them in bondage for generations. Acquisition of lands for industrial and irrigation or power projects had left many of them without a home or any source of decent livelihood. Cash compensations received by them for the land acquired by the state had been frittered away in unproductive expenses, characteristic of the tribal's nonchalant attitude to life.

With Choudhary Charan Singh

I organized a drive for on-the-spot trial of cases for the restoration of the tribal's alienated lands, which yielded highly satisfactory results in the beginning. With competent assistance from Mr. Ehsan Ahmed, Deputy Commissioner of Sighbhum, I intervened in a dispute between the workers and forest contractors of Singhbhum which secured for the tribals of the area higher wages and better working conditions. But, these efforts remained peripheral and could not make any major dent on the prevailing scheme of exploitation. Meanwhile, the Adivasi leadership continued to remain divided, leaving the tribals fitfully despondent and desperate.

When I joined Chotanagpur Division, Dhanbad district was in ferment. The labour situation in the coalfields, which at no time allowed any respite to the district administration, had acquired a new dimension with the recent acquisition of the coking coal mines by the central government. In the private mining establishments, the controlling unions would thrive by simultaneously bullying and exploiting the owners and extorting money from the workers. Their strategy was to enroll musclemen loyal to the union leaders in the muster rolls of the mining establishments. The musclemen would operate as the private army of the union leaders and also extract money from the workers in the name of subscriptions to union funds. The muster rolls included a large number of 'ghost' workers sponsored by the unions. Salaries of such 'ghost' workers lined the pockets of the union leaders.

As the process of absorbing workers of private mines in the state owned enterprise continued, Bharat Coking Coal Limited started screening the highly inflated muster rolls. The stakes were high and the unions mounted pressure to have their followers retained and weed out workers belonging to rival unions. Inter-union clashes became an everyday feature. The district administration was anxious to ensure proper screening to purge the unions of their armed retainers, but the BCCL management was prone to making compromises, possibly under some external compulsions or as a strategy to win over and establish friendly relations with one or the other union, which further exacerbated the situation.

The process of muster roll screening eventually ended. But, corruption under the cloak of trade unionism held the coalfields in its grip as firmly as ever. The tentacles of labour unions spread across the public sector coal industry and the evil designs of local hoodlums led to ominous consequences.

All this was happening on familiar territory. But very soon we were deluged by a tidal wave of events which obliged us to turn away from the familiar and begin grappling with a totally new set of problems that were catalytic and transformative.

Addressing the gathering on Republic Day at Ranchi, 26 January 1974

Waves Upon Waves and a Happy Ending

The students of Gujarat leading the Nav Nirman Samiti had started a movement against corruption in government, particularly those in high places, and its echoes resounded in Bihar. Lacking mature leadership, the students of Bihar picked on issues sporadically with scarcely any sense of direction. Anti-social elements found it easy to mingle with student agitators and gave a violent turn to events at the slightest provocation. After a police firing that we had to resort to on one occasion at Ranchi, I closely watched the conduct of the motley crowd that completely out-numbered the small group of genuine students. The crowd would form itself into small groups and, when chased by the police, would run helter-skelter into lanes and by-lanes, only to reorganise and emerge on the main street in the opposite direction. They appeared well-trained in the tactics of teasing and harassing the police.

But it was also heartening to witness the new awareness and confidence among the student community. Emerging from their protected college campuses into the rough and tumble of real life, they seemed to understand that the roots of the current problems lay in the prevailing state of corruption and maladministration in government. A group of students once thronged the doors of a conference room where the Minister was addressing officials — it was the same Daroga Rai about whom much has been said —demanding that he come out to meet them. I reprimanded them for this meaningless misbehaviour and secured an appointment for them with the Minister later in the day. When a small group of students arrived for the scheduled interview, we were present in full strength to provide cover to the Minister. The Minister was nervous and answered their provocative queries with sweet persuasiveness. Daroga Rai, who was otherwise adept in debating and dodging political hecklers, did not quite know how to face pointed accusations from those who were not his political fellow travellers and his nervousness could be attributed to his own unsavoury reputation. After a while, when the rest of us had had a real good interlude, I intervened to free the Minister from his tormentors.

Jai Prakash Narain now took centre stage and sounded his clarion call for pulling down the government, asserting the people's right to disown legislators who had forfeited the right to represent them. The students were the main protagonists of the action programme announced by him. JP's first advice to the students was to abandon sporadic acts of violence. We felt relieved, but soon discovered that a massive agitation programme aimed at paralyzing the government had been drawn up. Boycott of classes and examinations, 'gherao' of legislators to force their resignations, frequent marches to local government offices and the state secretariat in large numbers - one such was led by J.P. himself - and finally, the call for 'total revolution' shook Bihar out of its complacency. A civil disobedience movement on this scale with the illusory goal of total revolution inevitably led to coercion and acts of sporadic violence. 'Gherao's, 'bundhs' and police firings were frequent and all the energies of the administration were spent in grappling with them.

Predictably, the movement started degenerating in the course of the next six months or so as the ghost of Bihar's caste-ridden social order reappeared and began casting its ominous shadow all over again. We started noticing that the Kayasthas, in particular, were taking special interest in supporting the movement and college principals and professors belonging of this caste were conducting themselves in a partisan manner to make their sympathies well known to the student community. To the rest of India it may not have mattered, but how could Bihar forget that J.P. was a Kayastha? Despite occasional outbursts, the administration soon got accustomed to dealing with the student agitators in its stride.

However, with the approach of the summer of 1974, a new and grave emergency threatened to overtake the government. This was the general strike of railway workers called from the first week of May. The coal belt of Dhanbad-Jharia and the iron ore belt of steel and allied industries in Singhbhum that were served by the eastern and south-eastern railways were highly sensitive areas. The Government of India sent half-a-dozen companies each of the Border Security Force for both these two sectors under two Inspectors General. One of them set up his camp headquarters at Dhanbad and the other stayed back in Patna, placing a relatively junior officer in charge of the Singhbhum sector.

The nature of preparations for defeating the strike was such that some of those who were commanding para-military forces lost their balance and sought to strike a posture as if they enjoyed overriding authority over the civil administration. Not a few of the problems we had to handle were created by the intrusions and officiousness of the BSF Inspector-General camping at Dhanbad. I recall an instance where he issued instructions to the para-military force stationed at Sijhua to march through the railway workers' colony after nightfall. Fortunately, we came to know of this just in time to hold up the exercise until a Magistrate had been deputed. Indeed, we had a real job at hand to protect the district administration from being branded as a 'gauleiter'.

The railway strike was effectively controlled and it was as good as over within a fortnight, thanks to the alertness and imaginative measures taken by the district administration. Of course we made full use of the Border Security Force sent for our aid and assistance, but also made sure that no excesses occured. And yet, the prevailing climate was such that the state government and some top bureaucrats believed that the railway strike was effectively contained only due to the massive presence of the Border Security Force.

A month before the railway strike, a communal riot broke out at Doranda, a twin city of Ranchi, on the occasion of the Ramnavami festival. One procession carrying the Mahavir standard had swerved into a prohibited zone, a narrow and crowded street with a mosque at the centre. A clash occurred, resulting in the police opening fire by order of the Magistrate posted there. Two persons died and more than half-a-dozen were injured due to the clashes and police firing. As quite often is the case, there were early warnings which, if heeded, would have enabled the district administration to take adequate preventive measures. Fortunately, there were no repercussions on that day.

On the main day of Ramnavami the procession was to traverse the main road of the Ranchi town. The unique feature of the Ramnavami festival in Bihar is that processions taken out for immersion of Mahavir's standard display their prowess in wielding lathis, swords and other lethal weapons as they move along. Even in normal conditions, the atmosphere is charged with excitement and exuberance. Against the backdrop of a developing communal situation, a religious procession of thousands of armed men proceeding menacingly ahead was like a moving mass of dried gunpowder.

The Deputy Commissioner had been suddenly taken ill with high fever and I had to take matters in hand on the day of the main Ramnavami festival. When I consulted Major General Naidu, the Army Commander stationed at Ranchi, about calling out the army in aid of the civil administration, he advised me against doing so formally. Thanks to our social contacts, General Naidu offered instead to move his men in formation as part of their routine exercise through sensitive areas of the town. The drill having been worked out, I climbed up to a temporarily erected observation tower and watched the waves of processionists pass by through Ranchi's main street. After hours of planning and preparation, followed by longer hours of nerve-shattering tension, I returned home when everything had seemingly passed off without any incident. I had barely sat down with a glass of whisky to soothe my tattered nerves when news came on the telephone about stray incidents of arson in the market area of Doranda. Another message followed, again from unofficial channels, about movement of certain personalities, suggesting major incidents in the offing. With no time to lose, I hurriedly collected a section of armed police force in a jeep, along with a Magistrate, and rushed out to see things for myself.

As I entered that part of Doranda which was occupied mostly by Muslims, I found the entire locality abandoned and steeped in darkness. Moving to the *darji* mohalla on the other side, I found a crowd of men, women and children gathered in the open courtyard of a temple and the Muslims huddled together in the house of a liquor contractor, with all doors and windows firmly shut and the grilled gates at the entrance securely locked. Some gun shots had been heard already, believed to have been fired from the rooftop of this house. The sheer panic was so overpowering that one indiscreet act by an excitable person with frayed nerves would have been enough to precipitate a full-scale riot. I used threats and persuasion to try and send both the groups back to their own homes to restore some kind of normalcy. Failing to convince them, I mobilised additional police forces to conduct flag marches to dispel the panic and restore some semblance of order and confidence.

As we moved around on our rounds, we saw flames rising here and there. With luck on our side, we were able to reach the trouble spots just in time to douse the fires and also locate some of the sources of mischief. With selective arrests of mischief mongers on a moderate scale, by next morning the monster of a communal riot, that had threatened to ravage Ranchi town and surrounding areas, breathed its last.

At the end of this long narrative, let me break the story of how, in the midst of it all, I got slapped by one of my own officers. S.K. Saha of the I.A.S. had just joined as Deputy Development Commissioner and was still struggling with the problem of somehow asserting his status as equivalent to the Deputy Commissioner, under the new dispensation where development functions were separated from general administration and law and order and entrusted to an officer usually junior in rank to the Deputy Commissioner. As the Deputy Commissioner was down in bed with fever, I had Mr. Saha notified as an Additional District Magistrate for helping me during this emergency. With exemplary alacrity Saha caught up with me during my rounds of the affected areas. As we were moving around, we noticed fire emanating from a nearby building, descended upon the abandoned structure and quickly extinguished the flame that had probably been lighted just moments before. As we were leaving, I noticed an outhouse in one corner of the compound which appeared to be occupied and decided to probe. The policemen started banging at the door vigorously, but that was not enough to wake up the person inside who was feigning sleep. Eventually, the fellow came out looking suspiciously like one who, if not directly involved, was witness to the arson. Hearing his mumbled excuses, I could not restrain myself and gave him a slap. In a couple of seconds, I felt a smart smack at the back of my neck and, looking back I saw Mr. Saha pulling back his hand. As if to reassure me that I was not his target, he mumbled a 'Sorry, sir' and gave another slap, this time aimed straight at the face of the hapless victim.

A couple of months after these incidents, when they were a thing of the past, Mr. Menon one day quietly told me that I had done a good job of controlling the riot. Coming from Mr. Menon, a man of few words and much action, this was a fulsome shower of praise.

Mr. Menon was practically the last Chief Secretary in my career in Bihar. He did remind me, for some fleeting moments, of the glorious days of Mr. L.P. Singh in the way he provided unified control and guidance to the administrative apparatus. Despite his taciturn and rather shy manner, he left one in no doubt that he carried the full authority of the government behind him. The Chief Secretary has since ceased to be the institution he was in the heydays of Bihar. The politicians have ensured that the Chief Secretary can no longer effectively command the bureaucracy or provide protection and guidance to his fellow officers.

Early in 1974, Mr. Menon had received a request for my services from the Government of Tripura for appointment as Chairman of the State Public Service Commission. I knew the Governor Mr. L.P. Singh must have played a role in suggesting my name to the Chief Minister of Tripura. After giving it some thought, I agreed to accept the offer and took voluntary retirement from the IAS to join the constitutional post from 1st January 1975. So, for the rest my term in Chotanagpur I had this thought at the back of my mind that my career in the civil service was about to end soon. This also became my source of strength and egged me on to serve the state, where I had spent so many memorable years, to the best of my abilities. The opportunity presented itself when the government announced the universal 'campaign' for eradication of small-pox.

The campaign sponsored by the World Health Organisation was being implemented for quite some time as a routine programme of the Health department. But, there was no abatement of the epidemic raging throughout Bihar, the conditions in Chotanagpur Division being particularly dire. Realising somewhat late, the enormity of the task and how the programme was qualitatively different from the orthodox method of mass inoculation, the government placed the general administration of the districts in full and direct charge of the programme and nominated the Divisional Commissioner as the 'leader' of the campaign.

The first stage of the programme consisted of a surveillance to identify the source of the infections. This involved house-to-house surveys to identify persons afflicted with the disease. As there was general reluctance to disclose any case of small-pox in the family, thanks to ignorance and superstition, there was a risk that the survey might miss identifying all the potential sources and thereby vitiate subsequent stages of the operation. Unless the field formations of the administration were effectively mobilised for disciplined and coordinated action and a tight system of checks and counter-checks imposed, the programme would flounder from the very start. The work of 'containment' was taken up in the second stage, by undertaking inoculations in specified areas around the identified infection sources. The success of the innoculation drive was entirely dependent on a faithful performance of the first stage of the operation. With the first two stages of the campaign properly implemented, 'eradication' of the disease would follow as the end-product.

By now, the original Chotanagpur Division had been bifurcated, with three districts of Ranchi, Singhbhum and Palamau comprising the South Chotanagpur Division. My first task in implementing the programme was to motivate my Deputy Commissioners of South Chotanagpur Division and also impress on them of my total identification with it. The next task was to spell out the dynamics of the operation without leaving a single loophole. The line of command and control having being firmly established, backed by the powers given by the government to the District Officers to commandeer the services of all government agencies within their districts, overriding departmental boundaries, the campaign zoomed to a resounding start. Weekly reviews by the Deputy Commissioners, followed by monthly reviews made by me personally, in which the Deputy Commissioners and the heads of all concerned agencies took part, maintained the thrust of the agenda. The World Health Organization team led by Dr. Brilliant kept up constant vigil and the Tata Iron and Steel Company came forward with generous help, lending their medical staff and a fleet of vehicles for the operation. I took care to visit some interior areas to impress on the field agencies the paramount importance of the campaign and arouse in them a feeling of participation and involvement. All our combined team efforts could not fail.

In about six months the goal was reached and Palamau, the worst affected district, was the first to declare 'zero' incidence. As Dr. Brilliant recounted later, he heard a knock on the door of his hotel room in the dead of night and cautiously looked out. Standing before him was a person who looked like a 'sarkari' man, he said. Seeing Dr. Brilliant, the man saluted and dramatically announced: 'Palamau declares zero incidence of small pox'. The last divisional conference which I held after other districts had achieved zero incidence in quick succession was the last in my career in the service. On this occasion, WHO's Dr. Brilliant delivered a congratulatory message and gave away some token gifts in appreciation of our association with the campaign. Turning to me, he said that he could do no better in recognising my services to the campaign than to confer on me the honorific of 'Doctor'. It seems the Telephone Department had anticipated this, for its Directory of the Bihar Circle issued in July 1973 had affixed 'Dr.' before my name.

On the afternoon of 31st December 1974, I handed over charge of the office of Divisional Commissioner to end my career in the Indian Administrative Service. I felt a sense of calm fulfillment and none of the pangs of severance from the life I had lived for more than thirty-two years. I was full of anticipation for the new life awaiting me in Tripura, which for me was the land of King Govinda Manikya, hero of Tagore's drama – 'Sacrifice'.

My Parents, Prof. Nirmalmoy Ghosh and Nalini Bala

With eldest son Abhik and his family, Muzaffarpur

Ramola and me at Muzaffarpur, 1988

With elder brother and younger sister, in Ranchi

With my wife Ramola and our five children

In Far Away Tripura: A Fitting Epilogue

I am writing this chapter as an epilogue. Though I functioned in a completely new role in Tripura, my experience here reiterates the central message of my career as a civil servant. That message is that in the emerging ethos of our overly political society, a civil servant committed to the basic concepts of neutrality and fairness and canons of good governance derived from the fundamental tenets of our Constitution, has to face an unequal struggle with the political masters in seeking to uphold his principles and convictions. It is necessary to be reminded of this message over and over again, as a deceptive and distorted doctrine of a loyal and "committed bureaucracy" has already found currency among the cynics and opportunists of the service.

The mid-morning Fokker Friendship flight from Calcutta's Dumdum airport brought me to Agartala, the capital of Tripura, on New Year's Day of 1975. After completing the formality of assuming office as Chairman of the Public Service Commission, I retired to my suite in a wing of the Circuit House, which would be my temporary abode for some time. The calmness of the surroundings acted like a balm for my tired nerves and I felt a lightness I had not known for many years. I gazed upon the rolling hills of the Baramura Range, the lush green valleys all around, the paddy fields dotting the gentle slopes, and clusters of houses made of criss-crossed bamboo splints with tin roofs painted in shades of green and maroon. I was far away from the familiar world I had known all my life.

Three years went by, with the Commission trying to secure compliance with correct procedures and introducing regularity in the management of the state's public services, but success was only marginal. However, despite the reluctance and sheer lethargy of the state government to act in accordance with the Commission's advice, the status of the Public Service Commission as an independent institution under the Constitution was never in doubt. This was due to the tradition built up over many years by the ruling political parties which recognised the important role of constitutional bodies. Having observed thus, I was getting more than a little frustrated as most of our efforts to bring about some order and probity seemed to end with no results in sight. The Constitution meanwhile had been amended, raising the retirement age of the Commission's Chairman to sixty-two years, adding two more years to my tenure.

It was at this stage that the Communist Party of India (Marxist) was returned to power in Tripura with a massive mandate, winning 56 of the 60 seats in the Assembly elections held in January 1978. I attended the swearing-in ceremony of the new government but, until the time I proceeded on leave from the middle of the month, I did not get to meet the new Chief Minister, Sri Nripen Chakravorty.

I returned from leave with great expectations. The Communist members of the newly constituted Assembly were used to carefully studying the Commission's Annual Reports and made useful contributions in course of the Assembly debates. Their critique of the government for the flaws and deficits highlighted in our reports revealed some understanding of the independent and corrective role of the Public Service Commission. The Communists, moreover, had built up a reputation for personal integrity.

The first thing I saw on resuming office was a couple of letters received from the government during my absence which had been sensibly withheld pending my return. There were complaints about unfair discrimination from some unsuccessful candidates on which the government had asked the Commission for a 'detailed report'. On the face of it, such communications were so absurdly misconceived that I could ascribe it only to the inexperience of the new Chief Minister, who had himself made the relevant endorsement on one such petition. A junior officer had done the rest without applying his mind.

I now called on the Chief Minister and told him in rather plain language that the department concerned should have pointed out to him that a report of this sort could not be called for from the Public Service Commission as we are not required to 'explain' why in our assessment we had rejected some candidate as unsuitable. I would not, therefore, send any reply to the petitions on which we had been asked to report.

I came away hoping that I had made my point about the independent status of the Public Service Commission. But, within a short time, the Chief Minister endorsed in his own hand another similar petition, this time directly addressing the Secretary of the Commission, which was grossly improper. Not wishing to start a confrontation and considering, in particular, the situation of the Secretary who was an I.A.S. officer on deputation from the state cadre, I permitted him to meet the Chief Minister and again explain the position to him. But, dealing now with an officer of the state government, the Chief Minister insisted on a written report on the allegations contained in the various petitions. It was getting clearer that the Chief Minister's intention was to make the Public Service Commission 'answerable' to the government. On my instruction, the Secretary handed over to him an unsigned note to clarify some misrepresentations of facts in the relevant petitions. The Chief Minister did not feel satisfied and said something to that effect, but desisted from pursuing the matter further.

In the next few months, the new government made fresh attempts to secure our concurrence in some irregular promotions ordered by the previous regime where concurrence had already been declined. A most amazing thing now happened. An officer whom Nripen Chakravorty, as leader of the opposition, had earlier named and shamed for his alleged misdeeds and against whom several vigilance cases were being actively pursued, was appointed on ad hoc basis to a post in the IAS cadre. And this was done brushing aside the recommendation of a statutory selection committee which had removed his name from the select list of officers considered suitable for promotion to the I.A.S. Such extraordinary conduct, to reward an officer of dubious integrity, confirmed the general belief that he had made some private atonement to the satisfaction of the party in power. It served as an open avowal of the Communist government's established policy of politicising and bending the services to serve party interests, trends which were already visible with the subordinate ranks having succumbed 'en masse'.

One evening, the Chief Minister, Sri Chakravorty phoned me with a seemingly innocuous request. A reference had just been made to the Commission proposing certain amendments to the Recruitment Rules for appointment to the post of Assistant Engineer. He said he would be glad if our advice was sent quickly. It struck me as rather strange that the Chief Minister should consider it necessary to speak to me personally on such a minor issue. He made another call sometime later requesting that the Commission may expedite its recommendations for appointment to some vacant posts of engineers, for which requisitions had just been sent. In this instance too, there was no reason for the Chief Minister to follow up the matter personally with me. I soon realised that his main idea was to establish a direct line of communication with the Chairman and also to get some prior inkling about the Commission's views in certain matters. In fact, in the course of our second conversation he had offered his own views about introducing simplified selection criteria and norms which should suffice for all practical purposes. When I declined to be drawn in, he lost his composure and accused the Commission of being unresponsive and unmindful of the interests of the state.

It was getting clear beyond doubt that the independence of the Commission, which refused to function as a 'tool' of the government and yet which the government was obliged to consult and defer to, was not conceptually acceptable to the Communist Chief Minister who swore by principles of 'democratic centralism'. As I was getting prepared to take some decisive step, some developments quickly brought matters to a quick conclusion.

Allegations against the former Chief Minister, Sri Sukhomoy Sen Gupta were being enquired into independently. One allegation was that the former Chief Minister had exerted undue influence on the Public Service Commission to declare a candidate ineligible for appointment to a particular post due to the latter's political leanings. The newly appointed Advocate General of Tripura, a nominee of an important Marxist leader of West Bengal, examined the complainant before the Inquiry Officer nominated by the Shah Commission. He pointedly led questions to elicit the response that the former Chief Minister had 'used' the Public Service Commission to damage his career prospects. The government's case was presented before the Tribunal on the basis of the complainant's deposition and the Commission was left to defend itself at the next stage of hearing. The Inquiry Officer took the firm stand that the allegation against the indicted Chief Minister was not maintainable as it was, in effect, an allegation against the Public Service Commission.

The next episode followed without much loss of time. Some candidate who had failed to get selected for the Tripura Civil Service in 1975 and again in 1976, for which competitive examinations had been held, petitioned the Chief Minister making similar allegations of discrimination. The

Chief Minister promptly forwarded the petition in original with his endorsement to the Chairman "kindly to see". The Government was evidently sparing no effort to instill some good sense into a seemingly intractable Public Service Commission.

This time I picked up my pen and wrote back to the Chief Minister. I rubbed it in, especially for his benefit, that the petitioner was wholly unaware of the constitutional status of the Public Service Commission, which was "not an adjunct of the State Government". I ended this letter by saying that I was taking an unusual step in furnishing to him some information about how we functioned only in order to set the matter at rest.

The thrust of my observations could not have been missed. But, having done my part and realising that the Chief Minister had his own fixed ideas flowing from his own political orientation, I decided that it would do nobody any good if I continued in my post any longer.

Within a week I met the Governor and followed it up by demitting office, voluntarily cutting short my tenure in Tripura. So, on 7 October, 1978, I took the flight from Agartala on way to Ranchi, my adopted home, to settle down as a free citizen of a free country.